Birdscape

Birdscape

BRUCE PEARSON AND ROBERT BURTON

HarperCollins*Publishers*

in association with
Channel Four Television Company Limited

HarperCollins*Publishers*
London · Glasgow · Sydney · Auckland
Toronto · Johannesburg

First published 1991

2 4 6 8 10 9 7 5 3

© in the text Robert Burton 1991
© in the pictures Bruce Pearson 1991

ISBN 0 00 219923 8

Reproduction by J Film Processing, Bangkok, Thailand
Printed and Bound in Great Britain by
HarperCollins Book Manufacturing, Glasgow

CONTENTS

INTRODUCTION

by Bruce Pearson

WHY *Birdscape*? Over the years that I have travelled the world as an artist fascinated by birds, it has become clear to me that it is impossible to paint them in isolation. I have always seen birds as part of much broader canvases, never as detailed portraits isolated from the space where they live. To my mind, understanding birds involves getting to know the landscapes they live in. To take one example, the red kite is one of Britain's rarest breeding birds. It has a distinctive shape of long, broad 'crooked' wings and deeply forked tail. A kite on the wing is a fabulous sight. But add late afternoon sunlight as the kite drifts over a wood of old oaks high on a steep Welsh hillside and you have 'kite country' – the exciting mix of a superb bird and its wild habitat.

Moreover, there are extra elements in the total story of the kite that must be appreciated to understand the bird. There is the sad story of persecution and egg thieving, the hopeful story of protection and reintroduction, and the politics of conservation. I am also interested in the story of the landscape and how it has evolved over the centuries, especially how human activities have affected it as a habitat for birds. The red kite, it turns out, is a relic bird corralled in a relic landscape.

As an artist I find that knowing a bird is also about looking at the effects that the changing seasons, the effects of light and even the time of day have on the appearance of a bird. Some birds change their plumage and look very different from season to season. For others, they are transformed by backlighting, strong direct light or the twilight of dawn and dusk. And not only appearance but behaviour: there are the different activities – singing, feeding or roosting – that are linked with the changing seasons and days.

I feel that an understanding of all these elements makes the hours I spend watching and drawing birds a far richer experience. I find it interesting to realise, for instance, that a Dartford warbler needs gorse and broom to survive in its heathland home. Not only do I learn about the ecology of the species but it is a practical lesson that tells me where to set up my easel. These explorations of birds of cliffs and heaths, bog and fen, meadow, moor and wood reveal equally exciting mixes of birds and landscapes. Each expedition sends me leafing through my books and journals in search of information that helps me get this broader picture.

With the help of David Cobham, the director of *Birdscape*, I concentrated my ideas on birds and landscapes into a series of six television programmes that looked at choice landscapes and their birds, along with other forms of wildlife, and attempted to draw them, together with my feelings and experiences, into a coherent visual essay. They were not to be seen as a definitive or objective guides to these places, but more like a gallery where an artist, obsessed by the natural world, had assembled in separate rooms six collections of impressions, thoughts and ideas, studied details, questions and comments.

To draw all these strands together in a book, I needed help. So I asked Robert Burton, an old friend and zoologist, if he would join me on my travels in search of birdscapes. I knew from previous expeditions together that we shared the same pleasure in getting involved in a place, picking out items of interest and relating them to the whole. It was important that Robert should write from experiences shared in the field so that his writing would reflect the paintings, sketches, thoughts and comments that I would present in the television programmes. While I was engrossed with painting at each birdscape, tied to the scene in front of me, Robert wandered off to explore. In the evenings, we met up to compare notes on what had caught our imaginations. The result is a book, based on visits to the six places made in 1990, that mixes our rather different approaches – that of the artist and the zoologist.

Painting from Life

Sitting for long hours while I paint birds in their natural habitats is a method of working that I have developed through years of trial and error. At first I brought rough colour sketches and pencilled notes made in the field back to the studio where I worked at refining them into finished paintings. I would try to capture the original experience and sense of 'being there' that I had somehow managed to capture during fieldwork, but it seldom worked out. For all the information I had gathered about the birds and their backgrounds, that special feel for the sharp shaft of sunlight or dampness after rain, the bend of a willow whipped by the wind, or any other fleeting moment of light, movement and colour, seemed to dim or vanish altogether when re-worked.

The creative gap was frustrating, but the solution eventually became clear. Why not take the my studio to the birds, putting it on my back and heading into the landscape? I could try sitting there and doing as much work as possible on the spot.

This approach needed a lightweight pack that would accommodate all that I needed for a day's work in the field. Portability is important so I could set up my studio wherever I want, perhaps miles from the beaten track. As well as the artist's essentials like a light aluminium easel and stool, four or five different types of paper, paints, pencils and water, there had to be space for extra clothing, a fisherman's umbrella, a flask of tea and a Mars bar or two –

The Mark III portable studio

after all, I would be out all day, sometimes for 18 hours when I get really engrossed.

Mark I of the portable studio had its beginnings in Antarctica; Mark II was designed to cope with the hammering of overland trips through Africa. Mark III, the current version, is definitive, at least until old age or infirmity means that I have to load it onto a barrow or hire a porter. I made it from aluminium tubing and reinforcing plates, bolted to a rucksack frame, with a cover of tough canvas to protect the contents, especially the finished paintings, from damp and dust.

For the *Birdscape* project I worked in watercolour, not as a purist might, but throwing on lots of body colour, crayon, wax colours and pencil. This is a technique that lets me work fast, before the bird flies away or the light changes, without waiting for meticulously applied washes to dry. I have always been more interested in the message than the medium.

At a glance the paintings may appear as mere copies of nature, but they are attempts to show more clearly the features that matter in the reality of birds and landscapes, whether it is the power of a peregrine in a headlong stoop or the crying need to save a habitat from the developer's bulldozer. Art is not painting what you see, but painting what you want to make others see.

THE WINTER BIRDS

ONCE in a while the winter weather breaks. Dull days of wind and rain give way to a clear, settled spell as a high pressure system settles over the country. The clouds disperse to reveal one of those crystal winter days when the sun shines out of a pale blue sky. Its rays have no strength, but there is barely a breath of wind so the air is pleasantly warm. On days like these the temptation to stop work and get out of doors is overwhelming. Bruce and I put down brush and pen and head into the Fens, the region of low country bounded by Cambridge, Peterborough and Spalding.

The East Anglian fens are not a popular haunt for country lovers. There are few places to walk and the flat acres of black soil are devoted almost exclusively to growing crops of sugar beet and oilseed rape, wheat and barley, carrots and potatoes. The skyline is only interrupted by starkly functional farm buildings, power pylons, a few scattered rows of willows and the looming bulk of Ely cathedral. A local saying, perhaps apocryphal, is that 'any fool can appreciate mountain scenery but it takes a man of discernment to appreciate the Fens'.

The scenery is one of simple perspectives and lonely isolated shapes but the main attraction of the fens is above eye-level, where the vault of the sky arches overhead and stretches to the horizon. It is filled with an ever-changing pattern of clouds and, in winter especially, it is brought to life by the many and varied flocks of birds flying to and fro. The birds come to this spartan landscape for one reason: slicing through the heart of the fens there is a strip of land, which stands out from the surrounding farmland. It is man-made but offers superb winter landscapes of water and sky and amazing concentrations of wildfowl. This is the Hundred Foot Washes, better known as the Ouse Washes.

The Ouse Washes are a narrow strip of land between two parallel, high-banked channels, running dead-straight for about 20 miles and carrying the River Great Ouse across the Fens to the sea. After heavy winter rain, the channels cannot carry the water coming off the higher ground of Bedfordshire, Buckinghamshire, Northamptonshire and Cambridgeshire so the Washes are flooded to contain the water until it can drain away and remove the threat of widespread flooding on the fen farms. As the water flows away, flocks of wildfowl, waders and other birds gather to feed on the waterlogged

The massive, ancient bulk of Ely Cathedral looming over the fens

pastures and they can be watched with ease from the high dykes running the length of the Washes. The contrast between the wet haven for birds on one side of the dyke and the ordered arable fields on the other is stunning.

The Great Fens of East Anglia

In times past, the Fens of East Anglia were a vast wetland of meandering rivers and pools, with meres large enough to take fleets of boats and miles of reedbeds. Today, only fragments of this landscape survive to provide a stark contrast with the surrounding featureless farmland. The Fens were a massive sump where the rivers Great Ouse, Nene, Witham and Welland drained the surrounding higher country into the low-lying ground that, in earlier ages, had been a sea-filled extension of the Wash. There was no gradient to propel the water seaward through the Fens and the winter rains gathered from over a considerable area of the East Midlands sprawled out again, backing up and inundating the flat country until the water had time to run into the Wash.

For thousands of years the Fens were a waterlogged wilderness described by the monk Felix as 'a most dismal fen of immense size...now consisting of marshes, now of bogs, sometimes of black waters overhung by fog, sometimes studded with wooded islands and traversed by the windings of tortuous streams'. Outsiders had reason to fear the Fens. As well as bottomless bogs and uncertain winter ice, ague (now known as malaria) and rheumatism were rife in this damp climate. The fenmen grew crops of poppies and hemp to provide relief from their shivers and aches.

Poppy tea and opium pill
Are the fen cure for many an ill.

The Fens were the home of outlaws and hermits and of scattered settlements of folk who farmed the shores and islands of firm ground that were a few feet clear of the flood water. Here they kept their animals, which were turned onto the dried marshland in summer. They sallied out onto the Fens by boat and stilts and vaulting pole; venturing into the marshes and pools and along the waterways to crop a wetland that was among Europe's most productive ecosystems.

Huge shoals of fish and flocks of wildfowl could be found on the Fens. Eels were almost a unit of currency. They survived out of water, if kept moist, and were used for paying taxes. The Domesday Book records that Littleport had a fishery worth 17,000 eels and the monks of Ramsey paid the abbot of Peterborough 3,000 eels at Lent for the right to take stone from his quarry. Other fish could be taken to market live in barrels, or smoked and salted. When William the Conqueror was advancing on Ely in 1070, his spies reported a wealth of 'pikes, pickerels, perch, roach and sometimes greater and royal fish'. The last fish would have been sturgeon which are still property of the Crown when caught in British waters. In 1912 a sturgeon weighing 32 stone (200 kg) was taken in the River Delph. The water was so low that it was killed with a shotgun.

Of birds there was no reckoning. The 12th century Book of Ely describes 'the crane, the heron, the wild duck, teal and most savoury snipe, the swallow-kite, the swarthy raven, and hoary vulture, the swift eagle, the greedy goshawk'. There was also the secretive bittern whose booming sounded over acres of reeds and was once described as the spirit incarnate of the Fens. It used to be a common fenland bird: in 1843, a party of fen shooters bagged 20- 30 in a morning, but it had disappeared a few decades later. Another

OPPOSITE A winter scene on the washes at Welney

Wigeon feeding in front of a rising flood at Welney

typical inhabitant of the reedbeds, the reedling, sometimes called the bell-ringer from its clear musical little note, has also disappeared. According to other old accounts, there were also dotterels, black terns, spotted crakes, whimbrels and black-throated grebes. The Fens must have been a paradise for birds, including the millions of starlings whose flocks broke down the reeds in their winter roosts.

It is difficult now to imagine this wealth of wildlife. It can be expressed by the harvest that the fenmen took. A man could net a ton of fish a day, mostly pike, bream and rudd, and send them to London markets by train. Ducks were netted or shot with huge, long-barrelled punt-guns; ruffs were netted and fattened for the table; and skylarks caught on a line of horsehair snares set in the snow and baited with oats. A day's catch might be 6-9 dozen and the Lord Mayor's banquet once featured lark, steak, oyster and kidney pie.

To outsiders, wetlands were a 'waste' that ought to be converted into 'productive' land. This meant draining and growing staple crops rather than harvesting the natural riches. The Fens came under attack first in Roman times when it seems that the climate was drier and drainage by diverting and embanking the watercourses was a practical proposition for sophisticated civil engineers. Thereafter, there were sporadic attempts to tame the Fens. The 15th century Bishop Morton of Peterborough has left his name on a dyke or leam that runs from Peterborough to Guyhirne but the fate of the Fens was sealed when the Earl of Bedford was requested by Charles I to set up a group of 'adventurers', rich men who would venture their capital to drain the fens in the hope of profits from allocations of the reclaimed land.

The civil engineer charged with the drainage was Cornelius Vermuyden, a Dutchman from the nation with unsurpassed experience of creating dry land. Vermuyden had already been knighted for draining Hatfield Chase in Yorkshire and in 1638 he prepared his *Discourse Touching the Draining of the Great Fennes*. His strategy was to avoid the piecemeal network of small dykes and banks that had already been tried and found to be expensive to keep in repair. He planned a single channel to carry the water of the Great Ouse straight through the fens from where it entered at Earith to its point of departure below Denver, so by-passing the existing natural channel that wandered up to Ely and back. By this means it was hoped to achieve the objective of making the land 'fit for meadow, or pasture, or arable' all year round.

'I resolve' wrote Vermuyden, 'to imitate nature (as much as can be) in the Upland Countries for between the hills are meadows, and on each side pasture grounds or plough land, I shall endeavour to contrive the works that way, that there be meadows between the uplands and the winter ground of the fens likewise...For that the meadows will be receptacles for the water in times of extremity to bed on all occasions of floods, and so to keep the waters at a lesser height by far against the banks'. In other words, the meadows were to be emergency reservoirs that would store excessive water when the Ouse reached flood level and prevent the surrounding arable land from flooding.

Vermuyden first dug the Old Bedford River, a straight-line channel 32 kilometres long, to shortcut the winding Ouse. This proved inadequate for the task and some years later the New Bedford River or Hundred-Foot Drain was dug running parallel and about half a mile distant from the Old Bedford River. Between them lay Vermuyden's 'receptacles for the water' – the

Hundred Foot Washes. The inner banks of the two channels were left low so that excess water would flood the washes – the land between them – while high banks on the outside protected the surrounding land. Next to the inner bank of the Old Bedford River a smaller channel, the River Delph, was dug to collect water from the drainage ditches that intersect the washes.

This was not the end of the draining of the fens. New channels continued to be dug until the completion of the Flood Protection Scheme in 1964, but the creation of the Ouse Washes was the beginning of the end of the fens which now survive only as two fragments – Wicken and Woodwalton. The rich fen soil makes some of the best arable farmland in Britain; until it all blows away, but that is another story.

The Ouse Washes have, however, allowed a vestige of the traditional fenland way of life to continue. Winter flooding with silt-laden water from the lime and chalk country upstream has continued to fertilize the fields, each one known as a wash, and give the fenmen lush grazing for their cattle and sheep. These conditions also provide an excellent habitat for a wealth of bird-life, which while not so abundant or varied as the original fens, still remains one of the best places for birds in the country.

Traditional fenland farming has now almost died out. Changing society and economics brought pressure for the changes that have already overtaken other farming systems, and it is a challenge for conservationists to maintain these techniques and save the washes for the birds.

Whoopers landing

'Coming in'

Wild Swans

At some point, into the still scene of water and sky, there will appear a small flock of Bewick's swans – perhaps four or five great, white birds flying with powerful wings winnowing and long necks thrust forward. My guess is that they are a family group; an adult pair shining white in the low sun and their cygnets dull in their grey juvenile plumage.

The swans have come from the northern fringes of Siberia, east to Taymyr, where the Russians know them as the tundra swan. The cygnets had been raised in the four summer months between thaw and frost and they had been brought by their parents on their first long flight around the arctic coast, by Lake Ladoga and across the Baltic to western Europe. Bewick's swans only started to come to England 60 years ago but there are now 5,000 on the Washes each year. They arrive in late October and November, pushing westwards as winter weather spreads from the east, and stay until March.

Together with the Bewick's, there are 500-600 whooper swans, also from northern latitudes. The two species are not easy to distinguish in flight but look for the more goose-like appearance of the Bewick's swan. It is smaller and has a shorter neck and stockier body and, if the view is good, the rounded head can be discerned. In close up, the pattern of the yellow and black markings on the bill is diagnostic. The yellow on the Bewick's bill is rounded or squarish and comes no farther forward than the nostrils. On the whooper swan the yellow is a sharp wedge. When swans are too far away to see these characteristics, they are sometimes called 'wild swans' to distinguish them from the mute swan, which is a much larger bird and, especially when swimming, carries its neck in a graceful arc rather than more erect.

The best place to see the swans is at the Wildfowl and Wetlands Trust

A falling flood leaving behind a mass of silt and debris

refuge at Welney on the south side of the Ouse Washes. At peak periods, there may be as many as 2000 Bewick's swans on the refuge in one day. They can be watched from the comfort of a heated, plate-glass windowed observatory, or, if you prefer to be closer to nature, through slit windows in one of the other, more draughty, hides.

The swans make a delightful sight as they come in to land. They are at their best on blustery, wintery days when leaving home has not come so easily. The family party approaches the pool in front of the observatory, gliding downwind and turning into the stiff breeze. There is enough wind to support them on outstretched wings and lower them steeply and speedily to the water. At the last moment, each swan adjusts the set of its wings and, shooting forward across the surface, lowers its feet and slides to a halt in a shower of spray.

Soon, the family is lost among the throng of swans scattered across the Washes. Some swans are swimming in the flood, either riding at anchor or feeding, their long necks dipping under the surface and uncoiling back into the air. Others are feeding on dry land, in contrast to the heavier, clumsy mute swans which prefer to remain afloat. The Bewick's are searching for the leaves and runners of sweetgrass, marsh foxtail and creeping bent or the seeds of bistort and hair-grass. Their favourite is the starch-rich roots of marsh yellowcress. The cress flourished in the long, dry summer of 1989 and the swans love it, staying on the washes to eat it instead of commuting to the fields.

However, the main feeding grounds are not in the washes, which are used more as a safe roost. Scan with a telescope from the top of the dyke on a clear day and you will see groups of tiny white dots scattered over the green and black patchwork of fields. Over the last 20 years, the swans have increasingly taken to feeding on farmland. Unlike geese, which are viewed as pests when they descend in flocks, the swans are tolerated by fenland farmers. Some damage is done by puddling with their webbed feet but this depends on the wetness and type of soil. When the swans eat the remains of a potato crop rotting in the field, they are appreciated because this is a sanitary action which helps to reduce disease. Even cropping newly-sprouting wheat or barley is beneficial because it causes tillering. This is the process in which damage to a

The bill shape of whooper (left) and Bewick's swans (right)

grass stem causes extra shoots to sprout, and part of the normal farming practice is to induce tillering by rolling or spraying. Tests have even shown that a field grazed by swans yields a better crop.

Recognising Swans

Bewick's swans first visited the Wildfowl Trust (now the Wildfowl and Wetland Trust) at Slimbridge in 1964. Peter Scott realised that the 24 birds gathering outside his house could be recognised by variations in the pattern of yellow and black on their bills. He drew the bills and named the birds. Next year, 18 swans returned and he was able to put names to 13. These patterns are as unique as fingerprints and over the years hundreds of swans at Slimbridge and Welney have been identified, named and entered in a register. Identification by bill pattern is an extremely valuable tool for learning about the swans. We were shown a 25 year-old swan called Neptune and 8 year-old Bernie, who had turned up for the first time with a mate and had four cygnets to prove that it was a fruitful union.

Individual recognition makes it possible for researchers to study the intimate lives of the swans without disturbance. A similar approach has been made with other animals, for instance by recording the white markings on the tail flukes of humpback whales and the pattern of whiskers on lions. As years have passed, the life histories of many individual swans have accumulated, with some being recorded every winter from the first time that they appear with their parents to their eventual death.

The upbringing of most birds comes to an end shortly after they have literally 'flown the nest'. Many common garden birds continue to feed their fledglings for a few days until they can care for themselves and tawny owls continue feeding their young over a period of three months while they learn to hunt for themselves, but families of swans and geese remain together through the winter until the start of the next nesting season. The traditional explanations were that the parents guide the young on their first migration and introduce them to the best places to spend the winter, or that the parents are more experienced in watching for danger and will defend their young from attacks by predators. These are possible but the main reason is that the parent swans protect their young from other swans when they are feeding.

One of the main factors for a pair's success at rearing families is the social position of the male, which is largely determined by his size. Dominant swans are continually jostling others for the best food. This could be serious for a hungry subordinate swan because, if food is scarce, competition will be fierce and it may not get enough. Observations based on individual identification show that family parties are dominant over 'childless couples' and lone swans. Young swans are less likely to be threatened by other swans when feeding near their parents and so spend more time feeding in peace. Moreover when they are threatened the cygnets call loudly and their parents come to the rescue.

Bewick's swans pair up when two or three years old, although some acquire a mate in their first summer and males may remain celibate until they are nine. The first family is brought to Welney usually when the pair is four or five years old and their success at rearing young improves during their first decade of life. It seems that some time is required for a new pair to get thoroughly acquainted: a swan that finds a new mate after bereavement is unlikely to breed in the first year of the new partnership and the new pair's breeding success improves over the next few years. Some swans have proved to be better parents than others. Pangle and Poppylot, for instance, produced 40 cygnets in 10 years while others have produced hardly any offspring in twice the time. It is well-known that swans mate for life but Josh and Olive were a pair that showed divorce is not impossible in swan society. For eight years they arrived together, but never with cygnets. Then, one winter, Olive turned up with a new mate and a cygnet. Josh turned up later on his own. From what is known about other long-lived bird species, it may have been the failure to breed that prompted Olive to seek a new mate.

Ducks and Others

Bewick's swans are the flagship species of the Washes but in terms of numbers they are a minority. The Washes are the home of the largest concentration of wintering wildfowl in the country, and there are few places in the world which can match it. Sir Peter Scott described the place as an 'avian Serengeti'. There are 5000 teal, over 60,000 wigeon, 5000 mallard, 2000

A sleeping male wigeon

pochard, 1000 coot, 15,000 pintail and smaller numbers of shoveler, shelduck, tufted duck and gadwall.

The names of ducks are marvelously evocative of wild places; deserted estuaries and saltings, lonely places of mud and water. The names are so varied and so distinctive. Shoveler, pintail and tufted duck are obviously named but the derivations of the more singular names such as gadwall, merganser and wigeon are very unclear. Ducks are also the most decorative of birds. It is not surprising that Peter Scott chose them as subjects for his paintings, nor that they are kept as decorations in the form of 'ornamental wildfowl'. The neat shape of the head and neck of even the plainest duck is very pleasing to the eye but many, males at least, have a richness of colour and pattern in the plumage which is hard to rival. This is often shown off to great effect in courtship displays seen in the preliminaries of pairing which start in autumn and continue spasmodically through the winter. But the quality lacking from ornamental ducks that swim tamely on lakes and ponds is the movement of ducks scudding through the sky, bringing so much life to the winter scene of the Washes.

Where do all the ducks come from? A number of mallard, shovelers, tufted ducks, wigeon and pochard, for instance, remain to nest on the Washes and they are joined by garganey which are unique among British ducks in being summer visitors only that migrate in from Africa to breed. Most of the throng are winter visitors, coming from northern Europe and Asia. Their numbers ebb and flow because the pattern of migratory movement of a species is not a simple shuttle between A and B. The birds are restricted to their summer quarters by the nest but they are free to wander in winter in search of good feeding grounds. Hard weather on the continent of Europe forces huge numbers of birds across the North Sea to our milder islands.

Looking over the flooded washes reveals a pattern of ducks superimposed on the patchwork of water and land. One reason why the washes supports such a number and variety of wildfowl lies in the uneven ground and feeding habits of different species. Slight changes in water depth have a significant effect on the birds. Dabbling ducks – mallard, pintail, teal, shoveler and gadwall – follow the waterline and gather over hummocks to feed in shallow water by immersing beak or head and beak and sifting the water for small animals and seeds. They spend more time upending as the flood gets deeper, with each species being able to work in depths according to its size. Tufted ducks can feed with the swans because they dive to the bottom of deep water.

OPPOSITE
Some different wildfowl feeding methods. Top: reaching down (whooper swan)
Second row: Left, up-ending (pintail); Right, diving (tufted duck)
Third row: surface feeding (shoveler); Bottom: dabbling (teal)

A male reed bunting

Swirling 'puddles' of water give away the position of a tufted duck as it paddles hard to maintain its depth. But it could equally be a coot pulling up plants which it will proceed to eat when they are floating on the surface. Lightly grazed or fallow washes are preferred by the ducks because leaves float nearer the surface and trap seeds, insects, snails and drowned earthworms collected upstream and now floating downstream in the currents.

With the wealth of wildfowl so easily observed on the Washes it is easy to overlook the rest of the bird life. Both marsh and hen harriers put in an appearance; the former in summer and the latter in winter. The typical long-tailed form of a harrier quartering open ground at low level and, perhaps, dropping into reeds or long grass to snatch an unsuspecting victim is one of the sights to look for. Peregrines and merlins are winter visitors and so are Mediterranean gulls. (Look for a black-headed gull without white tips to the primary feathers.) Geese are surprisingly rare on the Washes but white-fronted geese and a few bean and pink-footed geese sometimes appear.

After sweeping the floods through binoculars for wildfowl and other birds, and enjoying the movement of the flocks and keeping an eye open for rarities, I like to turn my back on the open spaces and walk along the dykes to see what is in the thickets and overgrown patches. There are tits foraging for insects in the dry, rustling stems of last summer's reeds and a variety of small birds gather along the river's edge where the flood has deposited a flotsam of dead vegetation for chaffinches, blackbirds, bramblings and reed buntings to pick over in search of seeds.

The Black-tailed Godwit

The Wildfowl and Wetland Trust was not the first conservation body to find an interest in the Washes. The RSPB became involved when, in 1952, a pair of black-tailed godwits, a stylish, long-legged, long-billed wader, nested, unsuccessfully as it transpired, on the Ouse Washes. This marked a return of a bird which had not bred regularly in Britain for over a century.

The black-tailed godwit is a bird of damp meadows and moors. It was once a widespread bird in East Anglia, and the Washes must have been excellent nesting grounds after the conversion of tall fen vegetation into tussocky grass, its favourite habitat. But shooting and drainage pruned its numbers and, once it had become rare, egg-collecting hastened its demise as a breeding bird. After the 1830s British birdwatchers knew the black-tailed godwit only as an elegant winter visitor although there had been a few, rare records of breeding. Then, in the 1940s godwits began to be seen in greater numbers through the winter and there were occasional reports of breeding.

The return of the black-tailed godwit has a lot in common with the return of the avocet and osprey but it never captured the popular imagination as these 'flagship' species. In each case there was the extinction of the British population, followed many years later by a build-up of visitors and then the exciting discovery of a nesting attempt, succeeded by a period of secrecy during which a protection and conservation programme was consolidated. Nesting ospreys and avocets can now be watched from public hides but the godwit is too secretive to allow this window into its private life.

Black-tailed godwits in summer

In late May, 1952, a local schoolmaster startled two black-tailed godwits, which flew away calling anxiously. This was unlike the normal behaviour of winter birds and hinted strongly that they might be breeding. A short wait proved that they were. The birds settled and the female, who does all the incubating, walked into a tussock, not to reappear. The schoolmaster walked over to look and there was the nest with four eggs. Alas, the eggs were lost a few days later, probably to a crow, but he found another pair two miles away with three recently fledged young.

There was a chance that this was just another isolated nesting of the type that had been reported over the last hundred years but in the following year the schoolmaster found another three nests.

Success was jeopardised by the problems of crows and cows although the latter could be excluded by fences. Another problem was human intruders, whether unscrupulous egg-collectors or over-eager ornithologists, but they were kept at bay with a policy of secrecy backed up by a discreet watch. There were a few leaks in security but no harm was done and numbers of breeding godwits built up through the 1950s and peaked at 64 in 1964. Secrecy had paid off; nesting was not made public until 1958 and the locality was not disclosed until 1969.

This did not mean that the Washes colony was totally secure. In 1955 the river suddenly rose and, despite efforts of the schoolmaster to raise the nests on mounds of soil, the eggs were lost. Similar disasters have overtaken the godwits on several occasions and spring floods have disrupted breeding so frequently since the mid-70s that the Washes' population declined to less than 20 pairs.

The problem for the godwit is that its ecological requirements put it between the devil and the deep blue sea. It depends in spring on damp pastures where the peaty soil is soft enough to be probed for earthworms, but wet places are obviously liable to flood and endanger the nests.

The black-tailed godwit now needs conservation by management to provide the best conditions for breeding rather than merely strict protection so the research staff of the RSPB have undertaken a detailed study, first to define the problems facing the nesting godwits and then to find solutions. This has revealed that flooding from April to June stops the birds setting up territory and destroys nests, while later floods do not harm the chicks but prevent the grazing or mowing that is necessary to keep the grass short enough for breeding in the next year. Summer flooding also reduces the all-important supply of earthworms.

Summer flooding is becoming more common because of an increased flow into the Washes through improved drainage and urbanisation in the catchment area of the Great Ouse, which includes the new city of Milton Keynes. Meanwhile the water is hindered from draining away because of progressive siltation of the watercourses. This situation was thought unlikely to improve so the RSPB raised a mile-long embankment around a key nesting area. As luck would have it, the last two summers have been so dry that there has been no flooding!

Conserving the Washes

Until shortly after the war, the Washes and surrounding parts of fenland supported a small population of men who still made a living from the land. They fished for eels, netted lapwings, trapped and fattened ruffs and shot wildfowl with enormous punt-guns that fired ¾lb of shot at one discharge. Peter Scott has told in *Morning Flight* how he and a companion saw two pairs of mallards on a pool. While debating how best to stalk them, a man with a spade suddenly appeared from a low mound and started to dig. The ducks, about 30 yards away, took no notice. They were decoys and the man was a punt-gunner setting up his ambush. It was, he said, an uncertain livelihood. "But I'd rather be here in the boat nor out on the black fields with an ache in me back cuttin' beets all day": a sentiment that has led the fenmen to fight the draining of the fens over the centuries. The summer would be spent with sheep and cattle but netting, shooting and catching eels were often the only way of making a living in winter.

Josh Scott was one man who was born into the old way of life and had every intention of continuing in it. At the end of December 1947, he noticed that he was being kept under surveillance as he set his plover nets on the washes. It had escaped his notice that it was now illegal to net these birds, but this was soon confirmed by the London dealer to whom he sent his catch. Shepherding became the mainstay of his livelihood until one day in 1967 when there was a knock at his door.

It was Peter Scott with a proposition. An anonymous benefactor had given the Wildfowl Trust money to purchase 100 acres (40 hectares) of washes as a refuge. The best place was the land where Josh had shooting rights, so how would he feel about giving them up and becoming warden? He was the ideal choice because he understood the management of grazing and the control of water levels, as well as knowing the birdlife. Josh Scott immediately decided

Lapwings at the edge of the winter flood

to join Peter Scott, by becoming part-time and then full-time warden and forming a valuable liaison with the local wildfowlers and farmers.

Over the years, the area of the Ouse Washes reserved for birds has increased as the Cambridge Wildlife Trust, the RSPB and the Wildfowl and Wetland Trust have added to their holdings. They now own over half of the Washes, but it is a piecemeal collection of plots acquired as individual washes become available. Between them lie other washes owned or leased by gun clubs and shooting syndicates. Their effect is to concentrate the birds on the refuge lands but they have to overfly the danger areas to reach safety.

However, there are worse threats than shooting. There have been plans to flood the Washes permanently to form a huge freshwater reservoir. There have also been proposals to improve the drainage and convert them to more arable farming. The latter fate has already befallen the washes that lined other fen rivers. As the river engineers deepened and embanked their channels, so flooding along their riparian fringes has been eliminated and the seasonal grazing land has been brought under the plough. The Hundred Foot Washes are now the only extensive area of annually flooding grassland in the Fens and so the only area attractive to large numbers of birds.

Management of the wildfowl refuge is based on the regime of flooding in winter and grazing in summer. The two are linked because it must not be forgotten that the Washes exist as a flood control mechanism and the pastures must be kept grazed in summer to allow free passage of flood water in winter. Grazing also provides an income for the refuge and maintains vegetation that favours wildfowl feeding on seeds in winter and waders nesting in summer. The tussocky growth that develops on abandoned pasture is no good for the birds.

The RSPB has rather different aims on its reserves and promotes greater cover in the form of reedbeds where warblers, water rails and marsh harriers may take shelter but, as we have seen, a grazing or mowing regime is needed to promote good nesting conditions for waders. Beyond this there is little that can be done. Floods can strike at any time causing disastrous nesting losses in summer and driving birds off the washes in winter. While Bruce was filming, a period of heavy rain caused deep flooding and the huge concentrations of ducks disappeared. The water covered their roosting places and was too deep for mallard and pintail, that like dabbling in shallow water, and for wigeon, that like to graze in the swards bordering the flood.

The present warden of the refuge at Welney is Don Revett whose principal occupation is ensuring that the washes are attractive to wildfowl. The high-profile part of the management programme that is seen by everyone coming to the refuge is the lagoon in front of the observatory where the birds gather to be fed. A barrow-load of grain or old potatoes donated by the farmers is shovelled into the shallow water in front of the plate-glass windows of the observatory and the scene becomes a seething mass of birds, with coots vying

Studies of snipe

with ducks and swans to get an easy meal. This is only a token feed to draw
the birds onto the lagoon where they can be seen by visitors. It also allows the
refuge staff to record the ring numbers and bill patterns of the Bewick's and
Whooper swans.

The birds' main food is obtained on the washes and, for swans and wigeon
especially, neighbouring farmland. Don explained to us that his objective is to
maintain the ages-old management system of the Washes that has been
handed down from generation to generation. The summer grazing of cattle
and sheep provides an ideal habitat for the birds. The animals have to be
moved about the washes so that they are properly grazed and water levels in
the ditches must be controlled. In spring, the flood water which had been
held in the washes by a low rim is drained into the ditches by removing earth
dams in shallow channels called grips. Shifting an inch or two of earth is all
that is needed. The level in the ditches is then controlled by opening slackers
or sluices to let water drain into the River Delph.

Don's management work is limited by the priorities of the water au-
thorities' need to control flooding upstream. They may have to release water
into the Washes and flood the ground, which will cause disaster in the spring
and summer. Normally, Don likes to get the washes as dry as possible in
spring so the sheep and cattle can be brought in. The grips and slackers are
opened and the water is drained into the ditches and out into the rivers. But

then the aim is to keep the ditches filled with water to keep the ground damp through the summer for the birds, but also to provide drinking water for the stock and, most importantly, to act as 'fences' between the washes.

The Washes in summer are a completely different place. Instead of acres of grey water and lines of bare willows, there is lush pasture and the edges of the rides and ditches are lined with tall growths of great willowherb, meadow rue and meadowsweet, purple loosestrife, flag and stinging nettles. These are plants which survive winter flooding and form the summer habitat of reed and sedge warblers. Goldfinches come to feed on the teazels which grow through the willowherb in late August and swallows fly past at knee height, twittering to each other as they hunt insects caught in eddies around the lines of trees.

Both summer and winter birds depend on the grazing regime on the washes. Where the cattle graze, the grass remains relatively long and docks, thistles and buttercups grow to give cover to nesting waders. There are 400 pairs of snipe; their metronomic *chip-chip* calls and hollow fluting of their tails mixes with the bleating chorus of the sheep. Black-tailed godwits, ruffs and redshanks also nest on the washes but there is a limit to the ground that can be set aside for them. Some of the washes have to be grazed by sheep which

Studies of wigeon

crop the grass short to make conditions suitable for ducks. If Don gets it right, there will be 80,000 wigeon arriving in September, but they will go elsewhere if he gets it wrong.

The Prophecy

After Peter Scott had visited Josh Scott in 1967 and persuaded him to turn from gun to binoculars, he wrote a letter purporting to be from an enthusiastic naturalist to a similarly-inclined friend. It was dated 1975, eight years into the future, and its objective was to reassure anyone who thought the refuge would interfere with the natural scene. It is a remarkably accurate forecast of the way that Welney eventually developed, although the numbers of Bewick's swans are much higher than he envisaged.

'Dear George,' the letter ran, 'I thought you might be interested to hear of a rather fabulous day we spent yesterday at the Wildfowl Trust's place at Welney...The Head Warden, a splendid marshman who's lived all his life on and around the Washes, met us where we left the car at the foot of the steep barrier bank of the New Bedford River.' The letter is describing Josh Scott, of course, and it goes on to describe the excitements of the day. 'The view was best from the observation room with the morning sun behind us and a perfectly fabulous array of birds all around. Within 100 yards there were probably 2,000 birds and they stretched away along the edge of the flood-water as far as the eye could reach – perhaps 20,000 ducks...' Then later in the day, 'Far away to the south we saw the ducks rising in clouds from the edge of the floodwater. Soon we saw the cause – a Marsh Harrier was flying along the shore looking, no doubt, for disabled birds. Gradually he worked his way towards us. The Teal would lift like mosquitoes and flush out on to deeper water.'

And so the description of the idyllic visit continued. They had a most wonderful day's birdwatching and the letter concludes 'As we withdrew from the hide, leaving the birds totally unaware of our presence and therefore totally undisturbed, I was conscious of a tremendous feeling of satisfaction. For a day we had been in amongst the birds, yet few of them had seen us. We had watched them intimately for long hours without harming them or even frightening them. Somehow this was a proper relationship between man and animals, and the way in which this refuge has been planned and laid out to maintain and foster this relationship seemed infinitely imaginative and splendid.

'There was tea in the Members' Room with the glow of floodlights far out in front and a white line of swans lit by them. Mallard quacked overhead as we returned across the steep bank to the car. It had really been a superlative day – you absolutely *must* go there.
Yours, Bill.'

Bruce and I have been there many times, along with thousands of others. It is just as Peter Scott prophesied over twenty years ago. We may regret the disappearance of the great fens but it is still a delight to see so many birds living natural lives in the centre of such a large expanse of tamed countryside.

TWO

KITE COUNTRY

W<small>E WENT</small> to Wales on the hottest May Day on record. By-passing Ross-on-Wye and heading westwards by Abergavenny, we squeezed between the Black Mountains and the Brecon Beacons and entered a new country where the roads are forced to follow the narrow valleys. At Llandovery we left the main road and followed the winding course of the Afon Tywi until we reached the RSPB reserve at Dinas, deep in the Welsh hills.

The woods of Dinas cover an isolated hill set in the Tywi valley on the edge of the plateau of Mynydd Elyneth, known as the Welsh Desert. Never thickly inhabited, the few remaining farms are worked by men living outside the plateau. It is an area traditionally given over to sheep where rare species of wildlife have found refuge. One of these is the red kite whose habitat is a mixture of open moors and wooded hillsides. The kite nearly disappeared from the British scene and barely held on in this part of West Wales until a longterm conservation effort made its status safe.

Kites do not nest in the wood at Dinas but, as it stands at the junction of three valleys, there is a good chance of seeing them soaring in updraughts along the hillsides. The wood is the home for other species of birds, some that are common in Britain and others that make the long drive to a remote part of the country worthwhile. As well as the woodland birds, where the Tywi flows around the wood there are dippers and grey wagtails and, if you go early in the day before they have been disturbed, you will see goosanders swimming in the torrents. A tour of the wood will also give an insight into the history of the Welsh woods and their decline, and of the practical work of conservation that is needed to maintain their varied and unusual community of birds.

Our first sight of a kite was tantalising. We were climbing the side of the hill, keeping a watch through the trees at the sky above. The characteristic shape – like a buzzard but with narrow wings and a long, distinctly forked tail – lifted for a second above the trees and sank again out of sight. It was enough to confirm that we had come to the right place and, walking swiftly up the steep path, we brought the length of the hilltop into view.

There was the kite, gliding level with the summit by employing the faintest draughts to maintain height and speed with no more than slight adjustments

The Afon Tywi running between Dinas on the left and Craig Clungwyn on the right

to the shape and angle of its wings and tail. As we watched, a second kite appeared. The two kites set off across the valley, one in rapid pursuit of the other, interspersing slow, exaggerated wingbeats with easy glides, and making mock attacks, lungeing at the other, which easily dodged by flicking over into steep, banking turns. Like buzzards, kites will also circle in thermals, passing and repassing each other as they rise higher and higher, while calling with a buzzard-like *pee-oo*. Our visit would have become truly memorable if we had seen the pair perform the spectacular cartwheeling flight, in which they grasp each other's talons and spin through the air, breaking apart only when they are about to hit the trees. This display has been recorded in many birds of prey, but only a lucky few have seen red kites performing it.

We hoped that they would stay in the valley and continue to delight us with their flying skills, but our kites were rather a disappointment. With barely a wingbeat they drew away until they dwindled into dots and disappeared into the haze, but they had been worth climbing the hill to see. Ravens and buzzards share these hills with the kites and are also adept at using rising air-currents to carry them about their business, but neither bird can match the effortless elegance of the kite.

Winter is the best time to see kites. Unlike most red kites on the continent, Welsh kites do not migrate, although some move south and east across Britain where they may overlap with kites straggling in from the continent. In winter the population in the Welsh hills is boosted by the newly fledged young and the kites may be seen in places which they do not frequent at other seasons. They also form communal roosts at night and one of the best known of these is north of Dinas on Cors Tregaron – Tregaron Bog – where a prize sighting for birdwatchers is a flock of as many as 20, sometimes even 30, kites circling together as roosting time approaches.

Kites make use of four different habitat types during the year. For feeding, they range over the rough pastures of mountain sheepwalk, the valley farmland of small fields bounded by hedges and walls and interspersed with clumps of trees, and *ffridd*, the zone of marginal hill land which lies between the richer fields of the valley bottoms and the mountain heights. The fourth habitat is the hanging woods on the valley sides which are vital for nesting.

The kite's diet is extremely catholic, with animals as large as woodpigeons

A study of a kite's nest abandoned earlier in the year

Red kites

and half-grown rabbits and hares, but kites are not valiant hunters and generally take only easy pickings; earthworms and even slugs are not disdained and voles are an important part of the diet, especially in autumn and winter. Carrion, mainly sheep, makes up a large proportion of the kites' diet and its availability plays an important part in the conservation of kites. In winter, kites are most likely to be seen on low ground and they frequent waste tips, farm middens and slaughterhouses.

The kite's usual hunting technique is to scan large areas of countryside with the minimum effort by soaring in the updraughts blowing up hillsides or circling in thermals in the manner of a buzzard, or to glide at low level, quartering the ground in the manner of a harrier. It is quite a sight to watch a kite hunting for earthworms in a field of sheep. From a slow glide into the wind, the kite checks and drops, sweeping in an arc close to the ground and snatching its prize in its talons. It is not easy to see what has happened until the talons come forward and the head drops to take the dangling worm.

Kites start nesting early, returning to the woods in January with their life-long mate. Nesting places are traditional, a trait which makes the study of kites easier but also helps egg collectors. There is also a tendency for pairs to nest near each other, sometimes within ¼ mile, while other, apparently suitable, woodlands remain unoccupied.

In common with other hawks, but unlike the falcons, kites build a nest of

A kite flying along the edge of Dinas in the evening light

sticks, usually on a foundation of an old buzzard's or crow's nest and a lining of wool is added. Kites have long been known for the habit of adding a variety of odd bits and pieces such as paper or plastic. To quote Shakespeare,

When the kite builds look to lesser linen.

The eggs, one to three in number, are laid in early April when the trees are still bare so observation is relatively easy. This again has its positive and negative sides. The female is responsible for virtually all the incubation and so relies on the male to bring her food. She continues to brood the nestlings until they are two or three weeks old and large enough to demand the efforts of both parents in bringing food. They fly when they are seven or eight weeks old but they remain in the trees near the nest for up to three weeks, where their parents continue to bring them food.

Decline and Rise

There was once a time when it would not have been remarkable to have seen kites in any part of Britain and there would have been no need to cross the country in search of them. On the contrary, the red kite was once noted for its abundance. It was as common a scavenger in Britain as other species of kites are in many warmer parts of the world today. A visitor from the Continent remarked in 1465 that he had never seen so many kites as at London Bridge. They were so tame that they would snatch 'from the hands of children bread smeared with butter, in the Flemish fashion, given to them by their mothers'.

Incidentally, there has been some question as to which species of kite inhabited London because elsewhere the black kite frequents human habitation. But the evidence is in favour of the red kite. William Turner, writing in 1544, recognised two species of kite. One, he said, 'is in colour nearly rufous, and in England is abundant and remarkably rapacious. The other kind is smaller, blacker, and more rarely haunts cities. This I do not remember to have seen in England, though in Germany most frequently'.

At this time, the red kite was a valued member of the community and was protected by law. Like kites and vultures in tropical countries today, it was an important scavenger in the more unsavoury parts of cities. Shakespeare's audiences for *Hamlet* would have understood the allusion of:

> *Ere this*
> *I should have fatted all the region's kites*
> *With this slave's offal.*

Eventually, however, the kite's position was eroded. It survived in London at least until 1777 when a pair nested in Gray's Inn Gardens, and kites continued to nest in Kent until about 1815.

The change in the kite's fortunes was due to its habit of stealing chicks and ducklings from farmyards and, worse, young gamebirds from shooting estates. Its trusting nature and its willingness to take carrion made it easy to shoot, trap or poison. As game preservation spread over the country in the 19th century and the ruthless campaign against vermin intensified, the red kite joined other birds of prey and carnivores in a steep decline. It was extinct in England by 1870 and had been totally destroyed in Scotland by 1900. Only a remnant population survived in the wilder, unkeepered parts of Wales. At the turn of the century, only about five pairs survived.

It is difficult to be certain about this figure because there were few ornithologists and systematic surveys of populations were unknown. Also the report of 'certainly three, and probably five or six pairs – eight would be the outside limit' may have referred to the whole of South Wales, to the old county of Breconshire or merely to the Tywi valley. It does not really matter: there were very few pairs of kites in Wales and the survivors were regularly robbed of their eggs.

The last pairs of kites were confined to central Wales, where the oakwoods of the sparsely populated valleys and the wild moorlands above provided a suitable, safe habitat. This area included the upper reaches of the Tywi. Some landowners were trying to protect the kites, and in the 1870s and 80s they may have been increasing and were often seen over the town of Brecon. Then Scottish gamekeepers were brought in and their policy of vermin control was disastrous: nine or ten kites were killed in the spring of 1889.

The turning point came with a letter that set in motion the quest to save Welsh kites that continues to this day. In 1903, Professor JH Salter of Aberystwyth wrote to the British Ornithologists' Club to solicit members' interest in protecting kites in Wales. As a result the 'Kite Committee' was set up. Funds were raised and small sums given to farmers and gamekeepers to secure their co-operation, while some landowners continued to shelter the kites on their land. There was, however, little return for all the committee's efforts, although two kites were raised – possibly the first for 10 years. In 1912, ten pairs were recorded, of which nine nested rearing eight young, but a decline followed and the interwar years were disastrous, with scandals involving local police and even volunteer wardens attempting to sell kites' eggs. Very few young were reared despite a large expenditure on protection. For instance, in 1938, £340 (a considerable sum in those days) was spent on five pairs in the Tywi region with the fledging of only one bird. There were even suggestions that organised protection of Welsh kites should be abandoned.

After the War, however, the situation was transformed by the involvement of Captain and Mrs HRH Vaughan and a reconstituted Kite Committee under the main sponsorship of the West Wales Field Society. The number of young fledging rose to a record for the century so far of 15 in 1954. Disaster then struck in the form of myxomatosis. Along with buzzards and other predatory animals, the kites fared very badly when the country's rabbit population virtually disappeared. Only one young kite flew that year. The situation began to improve, but in the early 1960s breeding again failed. The decline coincided exactly with the introduction of the powerful and persistent poison dieldrin as a sheep-dip, which the kites obtained from feeding on dead sheep. The appearance every year of so much poison 'bait' on every sheep walk could have finally destroyed the kites but they still clung on and, once more, began the slow climb to a healthy population. However, nests were still being lost to disturbance and to the activities of egg collectors. If the Welsh kite population, centred on the upper Tywi valley, was to thrive extra protection, now organised by the RSPB, was urgently needed.

Bruce's first visit to Wales, some 20 years ago, was to take part in the RSPB kite protection scheme. Teams of volunteers were organised, mainly students or others with the time to spend an uncomfortable week or two staring at a tree deep in the remotest countryside. In those early days, kite protection consisted of pairs of watchers taking turns at a telescope or watching for torchlight at night. Bruce remembers the hours of inactivity as the birds sat peacefully on their eggs. Relief for the watchers came only when there was proof that the eggs had hatched. However, he does remember the pleasure of watching the male kite bringing food for his mate who was tied to incubation duties.

Numbers slowly increased and, in 1967, the population of red kites had increased to 20 breeding pairs, which reared eleven young. Since then, the population has climbed steadily. We have since heard that a record-breaking 63 pairs laid eggs in the 1990 season, 70 young were counted on the wing at the end of the breeding season and there are now about 250 kites living in Wales.

Unfortunately, egg collecting still poses a threat to the red kite. The essential problem of egg collecting is that it compounds the other problems facing a species. As a bird gets rarer demand for its eggs rises and its decline is hastened. Unfortunately for the Welsh kites, the relationship does not always hold in reverse: the kites are increasing, but so are egg thefts. When we arrived at Dinas on May Day, Tony Pickup, the RSPB reserve warden, told us that six nests had already been robbed. I was surprised to also hear that a pair of dippers, which Mike Potts, one of the cameramen for this series, had hoped to film, had had their clutch taken. One thinks of spectacular rarities like golden eagles, ospreys and kites being robbed, but collectors want the eggs of as many species as possible so common species are also at risk.

Nest robbing has taken a turn for the worse over the last decade; one kite nest in six has its eggs stolen. It has become an exciting challenge in its own right to raid a well-guarded nest, avoiding the electronic monitors, climbing the tree in darkness and carrying off the eggs. The thieves even leave dummy eggs, complete with messages of the 'Ha Ha, you've been had' variety, in the nest to keep the birds sitting and fool the watchers. The RSPB guardians have replied with the same trick. They put dummies in vulnerable kite nests and incubate the real eggs artificially until they hatch and the nestlings can be safely returned to the nest. The dummy eggs fool the thieves, and the parents.

Otherwise, there seems to be no answer to the problem of egg collecting. While we were in the Flow Country (page 57) we saw a family with young children walking by a loch where we knew black-throated divers were nesting. Their behaviour was not the careful movement of birdwatchers and we alerted the gamekeeper. He challenged them but they were completely unabashed and complained of the 'fine Scottish welcome after their 600-mile drive'! No action could be taken unless they were found with eggs in their possession. Searching for the eggs was pointless because they would have hidden them to retrieve at leisure, but we heard later that their confidence had been misplaced and they had been arrested.

It is good to know that two people convicted of stealing peregrine eggs in Scotland in 1990 were fined £6,000 each. (The maximum penalty is £2,000 per egg.) However, Peter Robinson, the RSPB senior investigations officer, points out that fines alone do not deter egg thieves and more effective penalties are needed. Edward III made the stealing of bird-of-prey eggs punishable by imprisonment for a year and a day, together with a fine at the king's pleasure, while Elizabeth I reduced this to three months' imprisonment but extended indefinitely until the offender got security for his good behaviour. The RSPB, however, recommends a less draconian amendment to the Wildlife and Countryside Act to allow corrective supervision such as community service.

It is the selfishness of egg-collecting that makes it so reprehensible. It is easier to sympathise with the vendetta that gamekeepers and farmers wage against predators because their livelihood depends on the number of animals they rear. Egg-collecting takes away the beauty of a bird that would thrill hundreds of people so that one miserly individual can indulge himself in private. Even if 99.99 per cent of the population are convinced that it is right to protect birds, there are still enough people in the remaining 0.01 per cent to

Ferns growing on the branch of an oak tree

A common sandpiper sitting in midstream

wreak havoc. The RSPB reckons that there are something like 500 keen egg thieves operating in Britain.

Despite the depredations of egg thieves, the major problem facing Welsh kites in recent years has been poisoning. They are the unfortunate victims of the war between shepherds and foxes and crows. Although it is illegal, the shepherds take a short-cut to solving their problem by putting out sheep or lamb carcasses laced with poison. As scavengers, the kites are obviously attracted to these ready meals. It is difficult to estimate how many are killed but Peter Davis, the RSPB's kite officer, finds one or two kites dead each year from poisoning and estimates that more than half the Welsh kites die prematurely from poison. Last year he found four poisoned kites in one week; two were lying beneath nests containing eggs.

Meanwhile, there are changes taking place on the kite's upland feeding ranges. Since the war the policy of every government has been to aid farming and reduce the reliance on imported food that nearly brought the nation to its knees in World War II. One result is that there have been major changes to the uplands, with losses of huge areas of heather moorland and the fringing *ffridd* country of grass and bracken. Support for upland farming in the form of subsidies has led to overstocking with sheep and overgrazing of the upland plant communities. The numbers of sheep in England and Wales doubled in

Red kite on the wing

the 40 years from 1947 and it has been said that sheep outnumber people in Wales by four to one.

The presence of so many sheep on the hills is invaluable for kites because overstocking leads to a high mortality and plenty of carrion, but it is a case of 'One man's meat is another man's poison'. The excessive number of sheep on the hills and their mortality benefits the kite's need for carrion but the over-grazing and improvement by reseeding that makes this stocking rate possible is ruining the habitat for other upland birds such as merlins and whinchats.

Nevertheless, judged by other rare British birds, the kite can be said to have made a comeback, but its protectors have been worried by a continuing low productivity. Average breeding success runs at not much more than half the Continental average of young fledged per pair that has laid eggs. This barely makes good the losses. The reasons for this are not entirely clear. Even after allowing for the depredations of egg collectors and unwitting disturb-ance by visitors to the nesting places, the surviving nests have a high failure rate. A likely reason is that the Welsh kites are a relict population living in un-suitable habitat on the western limit of the species' range. Continental popu-lations live in rich lowland deciduous woods near swampy land or broad river valleys; a habitat very different from the spartan situation in Wales where our kites have taken refuge. Research by the RSPB has shown that young kites are dying in the nest through starvation. If the Welsh kites can spread into countryside where food is more plentiful, breeding may improve. A series of late springs in recent years has not helped because wet weather at the hatching time in early May kills many nestlings. There has been no such problem in the marvellous weather of 1989 and 1990.

One cause for concern has been that the Welsh kite population may suffer from the effects of inbreeding. If the present 250 birds are descended from only five or so pairs, they will have little genetic variability and may have limited ability to survive and adapt to such hazards as changing climate or disease. It is not easy to assess this danger and a number of animal species have returned from the brink of extinction and successfully built up large, healthy populations after passing through such a 'genetic bottleneck'. However, to bolster the British kite population and increase its genetic variability, the RSPB and the Nature Conservancy Council have embarked on a project of releasing kites from Sweden and Spain.

In 1989, ten nestling kites were flown from Sweden and released at secret sites in Scotland and England. In 1990, a further 20 Swedish birds were released in Scotland and 20 from Spain were released in England. They spent a quarantine period in cages overlooking their new home so they could learn the terrain and the movements of their prey and they were released with radio tags so their movements could be monitored for several months. One of the Scottish birds has already flown up to the Orkney Islands and back. It is too early to say whether these introductions have been a success – two birds have already been poisoned – but there is no reason why new colonies of kites should not become established, as has happened with the white-tailed eagles in Scotland.

Meanwhile an improvement in the distribution of our native Welsh kites gives further cause for optimism. Their breeding success has improved and they seem to be filling in the gaps between the established groups and maybe extending into new territory where food is more plentiful. It also seems that the kites are changing their habits. They are becoming tamer and, for instance, hunting rodents and insects during the hay harvest. Provided that persecution can be kept in check, we may see kites spreading into the lowlands and associating with people again.

Welsh Woods

'Whoever visits Wales sees her nakedness' wrote a visitor nearly two centuries ago, referring to the disappearance of the oak forests that had once clothed much of the country. The same could have been written about much of England and Scotland. The open scenery of hill and moor that so delights the eye in highland Britain was once almost wholly forested. But by modern times only fragments of the original 'wildwood' have survived to provide refuge for genuinely forest species of plants and animals.

We hear so much about the extinction of species as the tropical rainforests are cut down, but we often forget the similar disappearance of wildlife when

our own forests were destroyed. Beavers could not have survived without trees even if they had not been hunted, and British beavers survived until the end of the 12th century in Wales, longer than anywhere else, and how could any of our woodpeckers cope without trees?

The woods that cling to the steep hillsides around Dinas and Gwenffrwd are relics of the virgin 'wildwood' that once covered the hills and deep valleys of the Cambrian Mountains, although they are a poor representation of the original form of the forest habitat. The dominant tree was the sessile oak, the species that is associated with the thin, acid soils of highland Britain, but is replaced by the pedunculate oak on the richer soils of the lowland south-east. The names of these oaks give a clue to their identification. Sessile oak has acorns growing direct from the twig, while pedunculate oak bears its acorns on long stalks. The distinction needs to be made because pedunculate oaks have been planted among the sessile oaks and identification is confused by hybridisation. The oaks in the 'hanging woods' of the steep hillsides give the impression that the sessile oak is a weedy species, with a stunted and crooked growth, but sessile oaks can grow to impressive dimensions. The problem is that these trees are growing in unfavourable circumstances and they have been sadly abused by Man.

History of the Woods

When the primaeval forest was intact, the small population of Mesolithic hunters and gatherers only had the ability to open up patches by axe and fire, perhaps to improve their hunting grounds as the Indians of eastern North America did until replaced by European farmers. Signs of their activity would have soon been swallowed up by new growth. The Mesolithic hunter gatherers were replaced by the more numerous Neolithic people with their advanced stone technology and technique of shifting agriculture. The new farmers worked in the easily cleared, open forests of oak and birch at an altitude of around 1000 feet. Large trees were ring-barked to kill the canopy and let in light, while small trees were felled. The area was burnt a year later, after the cut wood had dried, and crops grown for a few years until the soil had become exhausted.

The Iron Age marked a great step in the settlement and opening-up of the Welsh forest but the Roman invasion brought large scale clearance; first for military purposes – to deny the Welsh havens where they could escape to regroup and ambush their pursuers – and then for settlement. The pattern was repeated by the invading Normans in the 12th and 13th centuries. The armies of Edward I were accompanied by large bands of workmen to clear the forest. Three hundred woodmen and charcoal burners were assembled at

OPPOSITE Sunlight and shadows in the oakwoods of Dinas

A male redstart

Brecon in 1282 and paid 3 pence a day to fell Welsh trees. For security, the wood had to be cleared to a distance of one bow shot (about 250 yards) along roads; greater areas had to be opened up around castles.

This slash-and-burn cultivation continued into the Middle Ages when one of the stories in the collection of Welsh tales called the *Mabinogion* relates how the hero Culhwch is given the Herculean task of getting a wood 'uprooted out of the earth and burnt on the face of the ground so that the cinders and ashes thereof be its manure; and that it be ploughed and sown so that it be ripe in the morning against the drying of the sun'.

As the human population rose forest clearance continued but the estab-lishment of monasteries, especially those of the industrious Cistercians, led to destruction of the forest on a far greater scale. The monks not only cleared land directly for agriculture but, by introducing the sheep ranching that has had such an influence on the upland scenery of England and Scotland as well as Wales, they slowly destroyed the forest through overgrazing.

Food production was only one requirement from forest land; it was also needed for fuel and raw materials. To this end, the woods still remaining from the original forest came under management regimes that have left indelible imprint. The Cistercians managed, as well as destroyed, forests. They took woodland harvests in the form of sawn timber, poles, firewood, charcoal, bark for tanning, acorns for feeding pigs and wild honey. In principle, these harvests should have been sustainable.

The trees were managed by coppicing, polling and lopping. Coppicing consists of felling trees and leaving the stumps which quickly send up a number of saplings. With a large root system left intact, growth is extremely rapid and there is a very high rate of wood production to produce poles that can be used to make charcoal or in the manufacture of various commodities. Alder, for instance, was used for making clog soles. Sometimes, the new shoots are pruned so that only one is left to grow. This is known as singling and was particularly used for charcoal production. Coppices were often planted with standards which are trees which were left to grow to full commercial size and produce large timber. The trees in Dinas and other woods still show the signs of coppicing long ago: stout boles to the trees, where they were felled in the past, with one or more comparatively slender trunks growing out of them.

A variation of coppicing consisted of trimming the tree about 12 feet above the base so that the new growth is out of the reach of browsing animals. This is called pollarding from the Norman-French *poll* – head. The most familiar

A male grey wagtail

Studies of a male wood warbler proclaiming its territory with song

use nowadays is in pollarding willows. Trees were also lopped in a more haphazard fashion and their green branches left on the ground for animals to feed on the leaves. Elm, in particular, was so treated but even holly was used. Local people often had the right of 'lop and chop' for gathering cattle feed and fuel. They could also collect wood 'by hook or by crook', taking dead wood which could be pulled off the tree.

Management of the woods continued until the mid-19th century when coal replaced charcoal for smelting, steel replaced timber for ship-building and other construction work and tannin was sought elsewhere. However, long before the industrialisation of Wales, sustainable forest management had been in retreat. A growing population needed more food and it also needed industry for employment and to provide necessities and luxuries. Existing farmland could not support the former, nor the remaining forest the latter, so the trees dwindled.

The economic need for woodland management also disappeared and forestry now meant the planting of new plantations on open land or causing further destruction of the old woods by underplanting with conifers. In the patches of woodland that remain the trees are old and often show the thickened bole and multiple stems that attest to coppicing. There has been virtually no regeneration because sheep have been allowed to graze in the woods so any tree seed that germinated and sprouted its first leaves was immediately eaten.

So the woods around Dinas have been shaped by the industrial history of Wales and are now threatened with extinction through overgrazing. This would be disastrous for the red kite and for a special community of small birds.

The Migrant Quartet

May Day, give or take a week or two, is the best time to visit the Welsh woods. The leaves of the oaks are sprouting, the ash and alder are still in bud, and the scattered birches and rowan are in full leaf. Looking up through the canopy in early morning, while the sun is still low, the leaves are bright green against the pale sky and the fresh foliage is not dense enough to hide the tracery of twigs. In this condition, it is easy to spot the

A female pied flycatcher approaching its nest-box with nesting material

Male pied flycatchers display to the female

small birds that live in the canopy. This is the time to revive last year's memories and match visual identification of the different birds with their songs. A week or two on, when the greenery is denser, they will become invisible songsters or anonymous forms barely seen as they flit in search of food.

The Welsh woods are not only different in appearance from the eastern pedunculate oakwoods, the woodland sounds are different. The rushing water of the Tywi and the chorus of bleating sheep are the background to a babble of birdsong which is now approaching its peak. There are all the familiar birds: robin, thrushes, great tit and wren but also a suite of less familiar songs: pied flycatcher, wood warbler, redstart and tree pipit. These four species make a bird community that is unique to the western sessile oakwoods and form the main objective of management in the Dinas reserve. The four are migrant insect-eaters which had returned from winter quarters in Africa not long before our visit and were now busy with establishing their territories and courting mates.

The last to arrive and least advanced in the preparations for breeding was the wood warbler. This can be a very tantalising bird to observe as it is continuously on the move, singing as it goes, and its soft green merges with the new leaves when it perches. The song has been portrayed by a poet as 'little waves of pearls dropped and scattered and shivered on a shore of pearls'. You will not find such a description in a field guide: more likely it will say prosaically that it begins with a stuttering *tip-tip-tip-tip* which accelerates to a trill. The song may start on a perch and continue in the air or the warbler may land in mid-song and complete the trill with a shiver of the wings. Just as you get your binoculars focussed on it, it is off again. To add to the difficulty, if you are unfamiliar with the species, there is a second song of repeated notes of an intense sadness, more heart-rending than the willow warbler's incessant complaints.

The steep slope of hanging woods is a great asset for watching woodland birds. It is often possible to find a spot where the wood warbler in the top of a tree growing below you is on the same level as you and only a few yards away. Then you can watch it flying from tree to tree. It is more difficult to watch tree pipits because their vertical song-flight carries them high above the trees, but their rather strained notes are very distinctive as they parachute with exaggeratedly arched wings and spread tail that gradually close until they plummet into the canopy like an arrowhead. Watch carefully and you will also see them unobtrusively come to the woodland floor to feed.

Pied flycatcher and redstart are, on the other hand, easy to find and watch. Males of both species are as boldly marked as their names suggest; the pied flycatcher is black and white and the redstart's name is Anglo-Saxon for the red tail that it flashes in courtship display. These two species were already paired up on May Day and the contrast between the showy males and their drab females made their behaviour easier to interpret.

I watched one pair of pied flycatchers prospecting for a nest site. Their attention had turned to a natural hole where a branch had snapped and the elements had eroded a deep cavity in the timber of the trunk. The male drew the female's attention to the hole by flying between perches on each side of it and keeping up a stream of rather nondescript song. It sounds as if the flycatcher is trying hard to sing well but not succeeding (although it is more accomplished than the spotted flycatcher). The song has been transcribed into English as 'Tree, tree, tree, once more I come to thee' but like all these anthropomorphic renderings of birdsong a certain amount of imagination is needed, and mine does not stretch to this one.

At intervals my flycatcher landed at the entrance of the hole and squeezed in, followed by the female. What went on inside the hole can only be guessed at, but it must have been the avian equivalent of measuring rooms and tapping walls. It is a protracted business because the matter had not been settled by the time that I had to move on, but I did find a pair that had already taken possession of a nestbox. The female was busy collecting dead leaves; the male, as is usual with many small birds, did nothing to help with this time-consuming

Sheep are a vital tool in the management of Dinas oakwoods

activity. He was preoccupied with guarding his hard-won assets by chasing away any other male that came too close; and not only other flycatchers, tits and equally aggressive restarts are chivvied away. Presumably he could not guard his mate and help her build the nest at the same time.

Managing for Birds

For the pied flycatcher, in particular, the sessile oakwoods of highland Britain form their major breeding grounds. With the decline of these woods there is a potential conservation problem with the species and the RSPB has conducted a detailed study of the pied flycatcher's habitat requirements so that their reserves in western woods can be managed to promote healthy populations.

It has been known for many years that the availability of nest-holes is an important constraint to the numbers and range of the pied flycatcher. Putting up nestboxes in a suitable wood has a marked effect on the population and has led to a spread of flycatchers eastwards through Herefordshire. In the Dinas woods, the population has doubled through the provision of nest-boxes.

There is, however, more to managing pied flycatchers than putting up nestboxes. They must also have enough to eat and this requires providing them with conditions that favour their feeding habits. Unlike the more wide-spread spotted flycatcher, which in this part of the country is found around farms and houses, the pied flycatcher spends only a small proportion (about one tenth) of its time sallying from a perch to catch flying insects. Foraging is divided almost equally between the canopy and the ground and both sites have to be correct for the pied flycatcher to exploit them. The flycatcher hunts by sighting insects at a distance, so it cannot forage in dense cover. It therefore prefers well-grazed woodland where the floor is carpeted with short grass and moss rather than woodland with taller growths of bracken, bilberry, bluebell and bramble. Similarly, open, low canopy is preferred to dense, high canopy.

The flycatchers compete with tits for insects on leaves, especially for the caterpillars of winter moths which both birds feed to their nestlings. Tits, which forage by clinging to twigs and leaves and inspecting them for insects at close range, fare better in woods with dense foliage and tend to oust the fly-catchers. They spend the winter in the woods and can establish territories before the flycatchers return from Africa. The flycatchers then settle in woods with open canopy, high on the valleyside, which they prefer but the tits avoid.

Suitable hanging oakwoods are in decline, even where they have not been completely felled. In some, underplanting with conifers and invasion by syca-more and rhododendron have altered the structure of the woods and pre-vent regeneration of native species so that they are no longer suitable for pied flycatchers. Grazing by sheep also prevents regeneration and the trees become thinner until only a skeleton of scattered trees remains. And when these trees die, there will be no wood left.

Sheep spend the summer on high ground and come down to the shelter of the woods in winter and eat everything they can reach, including tree sap-lings. Some remain in the woods all year and continue cropping anything that puts out a leaf. Eventually new trees grow only on the most inaccessible boulder slopes and ledges or in the wettest hollows where only alders take root in the mud and rowan saplings find a foothold on the larger trees.

Fencing out the sheep allows saplings to sprout from the woodland floor but there is then a danger that birch and rowan will take over and form an understorey that crowds out the oaks and makes the woods wholly unsuitable for pied flycatchers. However, oak saplings will not grow if there is a continuous canopy over them. Regeneration only takes place where there are gaps in the canopy.

The solution to the problem of getting just the right density of trees is to control grazing. Sheep, Tony Pickup told us, are his most important management tool. They are used to prevent the development of the understorey that the flycatchers do not like but are kept under control so that they do not wipe out the young oaks. He allows a small number of sheep into the Dinas wood from October to March, sometimes later, to provide just the right amount of grazing pressure.

Replacement of trees need not be a rapid process. Oak is a long-lived species and each tree that reaches canopy height has to produce only one replacement every 100–150 years, so a wood with open canopy and bare floor is not necessarily in decline; a few widely scattered saplings are sufficient to maintain it in good order beyond our lifetimes, so it will continue to provide a home for both kites and pied flycatchers.

THREE

THE LAST GREAT WILDERNESS

YOU cannot go much farther north in Britain than Sutherland. This seems, to the ear, an odd contradiction but Sutherland was the 'southern land' to the Scandinavians who settled the north of Scotland. Sutherland county shares the far north of Scotland with the county of Caithness, named after the Pictish province of Cait. Straddling these two counties, and sandwiched between the mountains of western Sutherland and the low farmlands of eastern Caithness, there lies the Flow Country, a part of Britain that was largely unknown, even to many lovers of wild places, until a few years ago. Then it dawned on the conservation community that a huge wilderness area, some say the last great wilderness in the country, was being destroyed by a dense carpet of alien trees. To add to their distress, it was being destroyed with the aid of public money but for no public benefit.

The destruction of the Flow Country has been authoritatively described as perhaps the most massive single loss of wildlife habitat since the Second World War and, even more worryingly, most of it has happened since the passing of the Wildlife and Countryside Act in 1981. Not surprisingly, thoughts about conservation occupied our minds for much of the time that we were visiting Sutherland and Caithness.

The Flow Country is a haunting, beautiful countryside of rolling, broad sweeps of heather moor and bog, picked out with pools and lochs, rising to remote, rounded, often isolated hills and intersected by swift-flowing, boulder-edged rivers. It is not the cluttered, sharper mountainscape of the more fashionable parts of the Highlands. Different from anywhere else in Britain, the flows have been aptly described as akin to the Arctic tundra. Tundra is derived from the Finnish word *tunturi* for the treeless northern regions, which could cover a variety of landscapes but, from my experience of Greenland, I agree that the Flow Country has a definite Arctic atmosphere. It is the southern stronghold of birds that have a characteristically Arctic distribution, so that I found the sight and sound of many of the flow birds evocative of my time in the far north of the world.

The Flow Country has been this way since the Ice Ages. It is a lonely place where you can walk for miles and see only scattered sheep and a distant

stone-walled bothy. Until recently the flows were the preserve of the shep-
herd, stalker, shooter, angler, a few hardy walkers and the most fanatic of
birdwatchers. The few roads were abysmal and even now they are narrow
and winding.

You usually have to trudge for miles across rough country to find the flow
birds but we found a spot easily by following a single-track road up a broad
strath. At one point it rose over the shoulder of a small hill so that the floor of
the strath or broad valley lay immediately below us. The rough bog terrain of
muted browns and greens was studded with many small *dubh lochain* – black
pools – and a few larger lochs silvered by the low afternoon sun. It looked the
perfect habitat for the Flow Country's special birds.

The air around us was filled with the shrilling of skylarks and meadow pipits but, at first sight, the bog below appeared pretty lifeless. We could pick
out tiny shapes of ducks and geese on the distant lochs and then we became
aware of the intermittent voices of divers and waders. In particular, I was
straining to hear the songs of dunlin and greenshank. These are two very
special birds. For me, the harsh trilling of the dunlin is one of the evocative
sounds of the high Arctic. When trekking around the dry tundras of Greenland, I soon learned to look for the diminutive, black-bellied dunlin in boggy
hollows where its nest may be found in tussocks surrounded by standing
water. Although it breeds over much of upland Britain, the dunlin's stronghold is in north-east Scotland. I am not so familiar with nesting greenshank,
but only the keenest birdwatchers are. It breeds in the wilder parts of the
Highlands and Islands and has a particular reputation as *the* bird of the Flow
Country, but like the dunlin it is essentially a bird from farther north, on the
high moors of Scandinavia and northern USSR.

We were in luck. This short stretch of boggy ground held singing dunlin
and greenshank, as well as golden plover, and, even better, we were eventually able to identify both red-throated and black-throated divers, greylag
geese, wigeon and common scoters on the larger lochs. So, from a single vantage point we had all the birds we had come to see. As time passed, we realised
that the other half of the Flow Country story lay directly behind us on the
other side of the road.

Behind its high deer-fence a plantation of spruce stretched up the hillside.
The trees were well-grown, about 30 years old, and formed a thick canopy.
Judged by the volume of their song, the dominant birds were willow warblers
but we could see chaffinches, goldcrests, blue tits and great tits working their
way through the trees and, more exciting, siskins and crossbills. Once, a hen
harrier sailed by and disappeared up a ride.

OPPOSITE The timeless Flow Country landscape

The Waders

Waders are the main ornithological attraction of the Flow Country. There are not only good populations of widespread species such as snipe and golden plover and specialities like dunlin and greenshank but British rarities such as wood sandpiper, red-necked phalarope and Temminck's stint. Only recently, ruff have been found breeding in flows but, unlike those that nest in the Hundred Foot Washes and elsewhere in England, these birds seem to have come from northern Scandinavia, so strengthening the link between the Flow Country and the Arctic. An odd feature of some of these birds is that their usual habitat in northern Europe is forest-bog, where stands of evergreen trees are interspersed with waterlogged ground, but in the Flow Country they have adapted to open, treeless terrain.

There is no other group of birds whose voices are more evocative of wild places, of moorlands, remote shores and saltings, than the waders. In the lower reaches of the broad valley or strath we had driven through stone-walled pastures where oystercatchers piped and lapwings and curlews gave their familiar onomatopoeic *peewit* and *curlew* calls.

When the road led us from the tamed river valley into the wilder flows, we were able to listen for the plaintive, drawn-out *so-sad* of golden plovers and the rhythmic *chipper-chipper-chipper* of snipe, or for the bleating sound as air throbs through the snipe's tail feathers in steep dives, a sound that earned

A male golden plover preening

them the Gaelic name of *gabhar athair* – goat of the air. When we reached our vantage point over the flows, we heard the specialities: the harsh trills of the dunlin and the see-sawing *too-hoo* of a roller-coasting greenshank. The dunlin's song-flights are low level affairs in which the bird shoots up to an altitude of 20-30 yards and circles its territory while it sings, but the greenshank climbs until it is a speck in the sky and its alternate rising and dipping on quivering wings is lost in the mist.

Viscount Grey of Falloden, in *The Charm of Birds*, wrote that he felt 'as if included and embraced in the pervading sound of the sustained vibrating joy-notes of the curlew'. The same can be said of the songs of other waders, although they are rarely delivered so powerfully as the curlew's, but much of the magic must come from the association. When you hear a curlew, a snipe, a dunlin or a greenshank, you know you are in a wild, lonely place.

The waders are birds of two seasons. In winter they are best-known for the flocks, often of great size, that frequent estuaries and shores around our coasts. These disperse in spring and the same species appear, well-spaced out, on their breeding grounds which are often in the wilder parts of the countryside. Frequently, the winter birds are not the same individuals as the breeders because waders are great travellers and many birds that winter with us migrate to the Arctic to breed, while our breeders have come up from warmer countries.

Much of the interest in wintering waders has focussed on their feeding habits and how differences in bill length and feeding habits lead to the different species exploiting rather different sources of food. On the breeding grounds, the waders present an intriguingly wide range of sexual and parental behaviour, which ranges from polygynous ruffs in which one male mates with many females, through staidly monogamous ringed plovers, to polyandrous phalaropes whose brightly plumaged females court drab males and leave them to rear the family.

However, studying the breeding of waders has, for many species, proved a challenge as well as a delight. The birds themselves are delightful, either because of their bold patterning, or because of the subtlety of their camouflage. Despite their nesting on open ground, their nests are extremely difficult to find, although the search involves you with some fascinating bird behaviour.

Many waders tend to sit tight on their nests until you almost step on them. Then they flutter off the nest, giving you quite a start, and you automatically follow the bird to check its identity. You spin around a few times, following the bird until you can get your binoculars on it. You confirm its identity and then you realise, rather belatedly, that it is hanging around in a significant manner, circling or landing nearby while keeping up a constant scolding, and the penny drops that it must have a nest or chicks.

By now, you have lost the spot where it took off from. This is, of course, the object of the bird's behaviour. It has distracted a possible predator away from

A dunlin sitting tightly on its nest

the site of its family. A stupid predator will not realise that there is a nest there and wander away and even the intelligent human now has difficulty finding the clutch of eggs or motionless chicks, both beautifully camouflaged among the greens and browns of the vegetation. With experience, you learn to make the instant decision to forget the bird and keep your eyes trained on the place where it was flushed. Then the nest is easy to find, and what a thrill of pleasure you get at finding these exquisite eggs, neatly packed with narrow ends inwards so they fit tidily into the warmth of the parent's brood pouch.

Some waders enhance this distraction behaviour by performing bizarre displays to draw more attention to themselves and lure the predator from the vulnerable brood. The bird makes itself as conspicuous as possible by flapping its wings and fanning its tail, often showing off white feathers that are normally hidden. Sometimes one wing is dropped in the so-called 'broken wing display' or the wader scuttles along the ground with its tail depressed in the 'rodent run'. It is often said that a predator would be especially attracted to an injured bird or to a small mammal and so be more likely to abandon a search for the wader's eggs. To my thinking, it is wrong to give a human rationalisation to what is simply the bird's means of making itself conspicuous. Why should a predator be more attracted to an injured bird or to a mammal rather than a normal bird? If a victim is in range, it should attack. The most spectacular distraction displays are those in which the bird seems to throw a fit. It falls to the ground, flailing its wings so vigorously that its body is lifted into the air and its cries verge on the hysterical. No curious predator can help but be drawn to follow this performance and so lose any chance it had of getting an easy meal of eggs or chicks.

The intelligent birdwatcher, of course, retreats to a reasonable distance and sits down with binoculars trained on the wader. It soon calms down and runs back to the nest, settles down, and disappears from sight. It is then that you see how incredibly effective is a wader's camouflage. You can only pick out its bright button eyes and the shaft of the bill because you know that the bird has to be where you saw it settle.

At this point, I should point out that during our short stay in the Flow Country I found only one nest and that was of a golden plover which came off its nest at my feet and I immediately spotted the eggs. After a quick examination, I walked on, leaving the plover to return to its incubation duties before the eggs could cool or a searching crow could spot them. If I was to relate that I had spent a couple of hours tracking down the nest of a greenshank and had persuaded Bruce to come and paint the eggs – described as the most

A greenshank feeding in a shallow pool

beautiful of all waders', so surely an embellishment to this book – we would have been guilty of breaking the law. Under the Wildlife and Countryside Act, the greenshank is a Schedule 1 species which may not be disturbed intentionally at its nest.

As it happened, I do not know whether I even came near a greenshank nest. First, the song-flights which we heard over the strath are no guide to the whereabouts of the nest. Greenshanks defend a feeding territory in the bogs but nest and rear families as much as eight miles away. The nesting habitat is in the wildest country which is not easily searched and sitting greenshank will not leave the nest until almost trodden on. If you want to read about the difficulties of finding them, of the fieldcraft involved and the excitement of success, you can do no better than read *The Greenshank* by Desmond Nethersole-Thompson. My favourite anecdote from this book is of the Highland laird who ordered his stalkers 'grim men in kilts and tweeds, cursing profusely on wet hillocks' to locate greenshank nests on pain of instant dismissal. 'Whenever the angry line of moist gillies had successfully done its work, the head-keeper was ordered to report to his master, who always consumed, as a libation, a bottle of the best in the cellar. Then, the old Chief, arrayed in the hunting tartan of his clan, and with his eagle-feathered bonnet cocked on the side of his head, bowled and jolted in a coachman-driven dogcart, along the track nearest to the nest'.

The Divers

The flows are the home of black-throated and red-throated divers which are essentially birds of the Arctic. The British stronghold of the former is in the north-west of Scotland, while the largest numbers of the latter are found in the northern isles, but a reasonable number live on the flows. Both species retire to the sea after breeding, so they might be better considered as marine rather than freshwater birds.

The red-throat often remains attached to the sea for the whole year, even during nesting; many pairs daily make long flights to feed at sea and bring fish back to their young. The result is that it can nest beside small bodies of water, such as the *dubh lochain* in the flows. They need be only large enough for the diver's running take-off, but I have seen red-throats in Icelandic marshes nesting on such a tiny pool that they had to swim along a narrow channel in the marsh to reach a larger pool to take-off. The black-throat, by contrast, nests and feeds on larger lochs, preferably where there are small islands for safe nest sites. The trout in these lochs are an important source of food so the black-throat was once persecuted by anglers and their gillies.

This life-style brings dangers to the divers, especially to the rarer black-throat on its larger lochs. Their nests are easily found by egg-thieves, as we were able to observe firsthand, and they are unwittingly disturbed by anyone

A red-throated diver skims across the water as it lands

wandering around a loch. Wader nests are relatively safe because they are hidden in the vast expanse of uneven country and are stumbled upon mainly by chance, but the shore of a loch is the obvious route for walks by the increasing number of visitors to the Flow Country, while anglers cannot help causing serious disturbance.

A diver floating in the middle of the loch is safe but it is very vulnerable on land. Like other birds adapted for a submarine life, its legs are set well back on the body for powerful swimming but, where penguins and auks have adopted an upright posture to facilitate walking on land, divers are incredibly clumsy. They come ashore only to visit the nest which is placed as near as possible to the water's edge. To cover even this short distance is an effort.

When danger is first spotted, a diver will attempt to avoid discovery by literally lying low, with head dropped and neck outstretched. Then it slips off the nest and into the water where it immediately submerges, coming up again at a distance so that there is no indication of where the nest might be. Niall Rankin has described in *Haunts of British Divers* how he was able to follow a diver's underwater movements on a calm day because of the faint ripples forming on the mirror surface of the loch. Twice, the diver slowed and the wake turned into concentric circles to show where the head had momentarily emerged to check for danger. Divers have the facility to adjust their buoyancy and swim at 'periscope depth' so, like submarines, they remain inconspicuous and ready to dive in an instant. Unless immediately left alone, the diver is likely to take-off and will not return for some time after the disturbance is over. Meanwhile the eggs are exposed to the attentions of crows, gulls and foxes.

If the birds have not been spotted on the water, their presence is given away by their calls. The red-throat gives a rapid, cackling *kuk-kuk-kuk* as it flies to or from its nesting pool. Search for the tiny, but unmistakable, shape of the diver as it approaches high overhead and watch it land. I always enjoy the sight of divers coming down in a steep glide on undersized wings, levelling out and hitting the water, then sliding to a halt in a shower of spray. Their feet are set so far back on the body they cannot be used as 'water skis', like a duck or swan, and divers splash down on their breast. You may then hear the wild wailing and yodelling as birds of either species meet again and reaffirm the bonds between them.

The divers vie with the waders for owning the most evocative and splendid voices on the Flow Country and they make the long journey north through Scotland well worthwhile. The calls of divers have a wonderful and mysterious quality that has given them a place in the folklore and mythology of northern people. In both Caithness and Shetland, perhaps through a common Norse ancestry, the red-throated diver is called the rain goose and was believed to foretell rain. On Foula, in the Shetland Islands, I was told that it

Studies of a red-throated diver

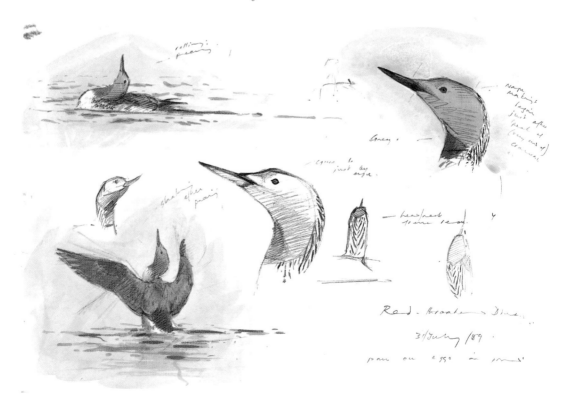

A red-throated diver swimming in the calm of late evening

calls 'We're a' weet – waur wedder' (We're all wet, worse weather). There was also a rhyme:

> When the rain goose goes to the hill
> You can go to the haaf when you will.
> When the rain goose goes to the sea
> All the fishermen go to the lee.

The *haaf* is old Norse for the open sea and the rhyme boils down to the simple statement that when red-throated divers head inland to nest it is time for the deepwater fishing season. Then, when summer draws to a close, the boats should be brought to their winter haven – a course of action which hardly needs a weather forecast! According to Edward A. Armstrong in *The Folklore of Birds*, prophecy by the rain goose of such mundane matters as the weather is the vestige of more significant beliefs held by many fishing people living around northern latitudes. The shamans of Arctic America and Siberia, who had close links with divers, were supposed to control the weather and conjure up storms, so forecasting rain could be a dim echo of greater powers.

The Bog Scene

Moor, moss, bog and mire are common English words which are used rather vaguely and often imprecisely for any open, wet, rugged and desolate countryside. They are also used as precise technical terms by ecologists, so a few words of explanation will not go amiss. (It does not help that some moors are called deer forests!) The most common use of the word 'moor' is for any uncultivated, open hill country usually shrouded in peat and covered in heather, as in Dartmoor and the North York Moors. The Scottish equivalent is 'muir'. Moor is also used for wet, low-lying places such as Sedgemoor in Somerset and Oxmoor in Huntingdon but the two meanings are not connected. The wetter moors are covered with a thick layer of waterlogged peat which is known as a bog, mire or, in northern England and parts of Scotland where Scandinavians settled, a moss. Extensive sheets of bog, called 'blanket bog' simply because they blanket the ground, are found throughout upland Britain, from Shetland, through the Pennines and Wales to Dartmoor, Exmoor and Bodmin Moor, but blanket bog is overwhelmingly the characteristic habitat of the Flow Country of northern Scotland.

The term Flow Country is a new one and will not be found in many books on ecology. It was coined by scientists of the Nature Conservancy Council in the 1950s from the old Scottish word for a flat, wet, bog or morass and they used it to describe the area of Sutherland and Caithness which contains large areas of blanket bog. It must be remembered that the Flow Country also encompasses large areas of drier moor and hill country so that 'Flow Country'

A short-eared owl about to plunge on its prey

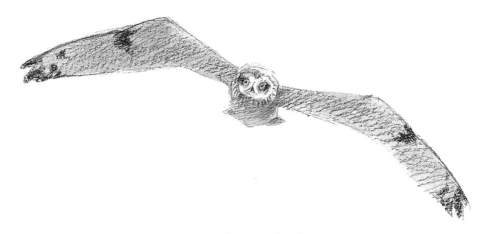

A short-eared owl

describes a region, while 'flows' describes the extensive bog habitat, distinguishable from the drier moors and fertile river bottoms.

The significance of the Flow Country lies in its geography and history. Blanket bog is found only where there is a cool, moist oceanic climate and the ground receives its nutrients mainly via the rain. On a global scale, blanket bog is a rare habitat and the Flow Country of Caithness and Sutherland is one of the largest areas in the world. Elsewhere in Europe, it is found in parts of Norway, the Pyrenees, Ireland and Iceland. Farther afield, it is found in the Falkland Islands and Tierra del Fuego, Alaska, Kamchatka, New Zealand and the Ruwenzori Mountains of Central Africa.

The bogs of northern Scotland date back to seven or eight thousand years ago when a rather dry climate over the British Isles was superseded by wetter conditions. Parts of the Flow Country, which had been forested, became swamped by bog, as is vividly illustrated by the blackened stumps of prehistoric trees that were buried in peat and we saw exposed in the sides of peat hags or the edges of newly-cut hill roads. It is believed that, to some extent, human settlers speeded the change by clearing the primaeval forest but there is evidence that parts of the flows never became wooded after the retreat of the Ice Age glaciers.

The last point is of great importance in considering the significance of the Scottish flows. They are one of the few habitats in our country that are natural and not significantly altered by human activity. The drier moorlands, which are often thought to be natural countryside, were originally forested and have been converted to heather and grass by centuries of felling and grazing. The blanket bogs have been damaged by grazing, burning and pollution, but they are now threatened with obliteration by tree planting. This wilderness of many millions of acres is set to follow another natural habitat, the East Anglian fens, into near oblivion.

Bog vegetation contains many species of plants such as Sphagnum, reindeer moss and sundews

The Bog Ecosystem

On a foundation of glaciated landscape, where rounded piles of rock debris known as drumlins and eskers remain as 'fossils' of ancient icecaps, acres of bog have built up layers of peat through the continuing growth and partial decomposition of *Sphagnum* or bogmoss. At a distance, the scene looks unpromising but bogmoss, itself, is an interesting plant and it shelters many others, especially in and around the many *dubh lochain*. There is bogbean, bog myrtle, bog asphodel, bladderwort and sundew, and on wetter patches of bog and surrounding the pools there are shining-white sheets of bogcotton or cotton-grass.

Looking around at the quaking ground as we squelched through it, I noted in passing how amazing it was that anyone would want to plant anything in it, but the striking feature was the remarkable variety in the colours. Bruce interpreted them as burnt sienna, ochre, olive and acidic green. These colours underlie the story of an interesting ecosystem based on one plant: bogmoss. Its most familiar form is a dried, fibrous substance bought as Irish peat moss at garden centres, although it is just as likely to have come from Sedgemoor in Somerset or Thorne Moor in Yorkshire as from Ireland.

The way across the wetter parts of the bog is to pick a circuitous route along the higher parts. It is not easy and it is often necessary to retrace your track and find a path around a maze of pools. It is unwise to try a short-cut: the peat in the pools is in such fine suspension that they appear bottomless. (Peat-stained socks and trousers are a certainty but remember the fate of Stapleton in the Grimpen Marsh in *The Hound of the Baskervilles*!) So stop on a solid patch before you take a closer look at the structure of the bog. It is more complex, colourful and interesting than it appears from a distance.

In life, bogmoss is a delicate plant with unusual properties. It has a weak, floppy stem and stays upright because neighbouring plants support each other in clumps. Within the stem there are open spaces which hold water like a sponge and contribute to the general soggy nature of bogs. In past times, bogmoss has been harvested and dried for use in absorbent wound dressings. As a bogmoss plant grows from the tip, so the other end of the stem dies and partly decomposes to form peat. The result is that the bog slowly rises but the process is uneven and the surface is a mosaic of hummocks and pools. When the bog started to form thousands of years ago, the bogmoss received nutrient-bearing water flowing from neighbouring ground, but the upward development of the bog cuts the growing plants off from the ground water and they have to rely on rain water. There is no shortage of rain in north Scotland and the ground is always waterlogged but it is desperately short of nutrients for growth and only plants that can tolerate such adverse conditions will survive.

The black pools may be studded with pale-stemmed sedges and spikes of pink and white bogbean flowers. The hollows are brilliant green with semi-aquatic *Sphagnum cuspidatum* that is replaced by blunt-leaved, yellowish *Sphagnum papillosum* and it is dry enough for sedges, such as bogcotton and deer sedge, and bog asphodel and cross-leaved heath. The perceptive botanist will notice that common bogcotton grows above narrow-leaved bogcotton. Higher and drier still, there is red *Sphagnum rubellum*, heather, twiggy, aromatic bog myrtle and the lichen *Cladonia*, known as reindeer moss.

As the bogmoss in the hollow grows on its dead remains, it dries out and the species change. Peat builds up and land plants take over until the hollow becomes a hummock. Meanwhile, the original hummocks that surrounded the hollow have dried out and stopped growing, so they are overtaken and become hollows in their turn. The process is very slow and there will not be more than half-a-dozen cycles of hollow and hummock in the thickest bogs.

Feeding its young is a full time occupation for a male wheatear

A Sad History

All around the country, birds and landscapes are under threat but the Flow Country has excited the attention of conservationists and turned into a battleground. The conservationists have two reasons for complaint. The Flow Country is one of the largest stretches of a habitat that is rare in global terms and it holds internationally important numbers of several rare birds in a unique collection of species. Unless large tracts are preserved, both habitat and birds, an unrivalled entity will be lost.

The problem facing the Flow Country is that it has for long been an unproductive desert supporting a sparse human population. The Ordnance Survey maps show an intriguing number of prehistoric remains: standing stones, cairns and hut circles. These are the ruins of the Picts, a shadowy but once thriving people who lived in northern Scotland. They were called *Picti* – the painted people – by the Romans and were believed, until quite recently, to be dwarfish people who lived underground. In reality, they were normal Iron Age people with well-developed artistic skills but who left few records of their lives. The Pictish culture was gradually replaced by the Scots from the west and south and the Vikings from the north and their country eventually became part of modern Scotland.

Life, and the human impact on the environment, changed little for almost 2000 years, until the Coming of the Sheep. In the early part of the 19th century large areas of the Scottish Highlands were cleared of their crofting population, infamously by the 1st Duke of Sutherland, and given over to sheep farmers. The sociological consequences are that the region has the lowest population density in Britain and you can walk all day and see no sign of habitation save, perhaps, for a desolate bothy or the fallen walls of a long abandoned hamlet where a break in the peat allowed a little cultivation.

The sheep, although comparative newcomers, are now seen as the mainstay of the traditional Highland way of life, but they have altered the vegetation by their selective grazing. They prevented the regeneration of trees, promoted the invasion of the hillsides with bracken and the deterioration of the most nutritious herbage. Into this declining countryside came the wealth of the Victorian age to turn it into a playground for the rich. Money acquired from the growing empire built wildly elaborate mock castles of the so-called Scots baronial style, where the privileged could live in luxury in the middle of nowhere and sally forth to stalk deer, shoot grouse and fish for trout and salmon.

Apart from burning heather to improve the habitat for grouse and waging war on their predators, sporting interests did little to modify the countryside of the Flow Country and its wildlife. While Bruce was painting, I spent some time wandering over a nearby estate run on traditional lines with income from four sources: sheep, deer, grouse and fish, and where the only wildlife actively persecuted are foxes and crows. As I walked the hills, my path was lined with alert golden plovers and grouse were popping up every few minutes. I also had marvellous views of golden eagles and merlins. If this century-old use of the country has had an effect on the ecosystem of the Flow Country, it was obvious only to a botanist studying the fine details of the vegetation that were lost on me. The bird life was clearly thriving.

There are two problems associated with this use of the Flow Country. In an understandable effort to rear the maximum number of grouse for the guns, keepers are tempted to break the law by destroying hen harriers and other birds-of-prey. Every year, the RSPB reports harriers shot and eggs or nestlings trampled to death. Whether such predator control affects the size of the prey population in the long term is doubtful, but if a harrier is seen taking young grouse it is hard to argue that its removal will not benefit the remaining grouse. However, it is interesting that the keeper we befriended assured us that he left harriers alone. He had examined their pellets and found that they were feeding on songbirds. Foxes and crows were his enemies.

The second worry is the growth of hill roads and the use of off-road vehicles (ORVs) which are opening up remote areas. One might ask why shepherds and gillies should not share the easier, mechanised life that the rest of us enjoy but Des Thompson tells me that the Nethersole-Thompson family's long-term studies of greenshank are showing that even this slight change in highland lifestyle can have a surprisingly profound effect on the flow habitat and its birds. They have found that the numbers of greenshank in one valley in north-west Sutherland have been falling since the mid-1970s. At least part of the reason is that ORVs are damaging the pool and hummock system of the flows. The bogmosses and other plants are disappearing, so there is less invertebrate food and cover for the greenshank chicks.

The Advance of the Trees

I was eventually thankful to find one of these new hill roads. I had walked further than planned across the flows and the road gave me an easy walk instead of an energy-sapping trudge over the hills and through the bogs. Whenever my meandering in the hills had given me a sweeping view of surrounding country I could see the sea-change that is overtaking the Flow Country. The metaphor is apt: conifer plantations are advancing across the land like the rising tide, first a pool forms here, then a wave surges in there, until the transformation is complete.

Since 1924, 1 million hectares of upland Britain have been planted with trees, mainly alien conifers, and around 16 per cent of the Flow Country has been planted, or is planned to be planted.

Until a few years ago, the notion of planting forests in the Flow Country would have been useful as a definition of the ridiculous but technological advances in forestry practice have made it possible and the turning over of large areas of Flow Country to commercial forestry has become a scandal to conservationists. Two aspects of the subject roused my interest and concern.

The first is the effect of these new plantations have on the unique wildlife of the flows. I once lived in Argyll, where the country had already disappeared under conifer plantations but I could see more birds if I walked through stands of well-established spruce and larch than if I walked over open hill country. A day's walk in the hills might yield only pipits, a wren or two and some distant crows or gulls, but it was worth the effort because there was a chance of a golden eagle, a peregrine or a ring ouzel. In other words, the open hills were tenanted by the rare and interesting birds which are unable to survive in the plantations, where a woodland avifauna takes over.

This encroachment on the habitat of the special upland birds has been described many times. Some species have undoubtedly benefited from the

A male hen harrier flying along the edge of a plantation

spread of trees. Hen harriers, short-eared owls and merlins thrive on the small birds and mammals that live in the coarse herbage of new plantations. Siskins live in older trees, but most of the birds are common or garden species and the new forests have little conservation value. On the other hand, foxes, crows and stoats thrive in the plantations to the detriment of the ground-nesting waders outside, as well as grouse – forestry is not popular with keepers!

Plantations attract some birds, such as this short-eared owl

The debate on the fate of the Flow Country has also focussed attention on the wider effects of plantation, beyond the limit of the furrows and lines of trees. Drainage upsets the normal water relations of the surrounding country so that it dries out and robs the birds of their preferred habitat. Moreover, the ground beyond the planting is no longer burned to promote fresh heather growth for grouse, and the sheep are removed. The herbage becomes rank and dunlin and golden plover, which like short vegetation, disappear. The plantations also fragment the flow habitat so that birds which require large territories, such as golden eagle, raven and buzzard, can no longer make a good living.

Another worry is that afforestation is doing more than drive the birds away from the neighbourhood. It is having a far-reaching impact on the whole environment of the region through its effect on the rivers and lochs. An immediate and obvious consequence of the drains which are ploughed in close parallel lines across the land before planting starts is that the watercourses are subject to flash floods. The flows once acted as gigantic sponges, holding rain water and releasing it gradually, now they are being turned into collanders. The water rushes out and the streams dry up.

Bruce Sandison, an angling writer who has been fishing Sutherland waters for 50 years, took us to a loch where he could once wade across safely because he could see the stones on the bottom. Not now; spates from the plantations have turned it into a sink of conifer needles and silt. He pointed out that spates can have a serious effect on the salmon redds, their nests in the gravel beds in fast-flowing streams. They may be washed away completely or covered in silt. Floods following spates are also a danger to divers nesting on the banks of lochs surrounded by newly ploughed drains.

The plantations also affect the region's water in a more insidious way. The rivers of the Flow Country may look like the pristine streams that appear in advertisements extolling pure, clear and natural products but they are dying by degrees like the blighted, polluted rivers of lowland Britain. The plantations have led to an acidification of the rivers, although the problem is more severe in other parts of Britain. It has to be said, however, that acidification is hardly the fault of the foresters and it would have taken place if the region had been covered with native forest.

Acid rain is the product of the waste gases from our industrialised and mechanised civilisation and the millions of needles on each tree act as a natural filter for toxic chemicals borne on the wind from distant industrial regions. Sometimes the concentration is so great that the eyes smart. The rain then washes the chemicals off the leaves, converting them into sulphuric and nitric acids and carrying them through the soil. There they react with the inorganic matrix of the soil to release aluminium. This is the killer when it is flushed into rivers. Aluminium kills invertebrates, as well as fishes when it penetrates their gills in sufficient concentrations. Without invertebrates, there can be no fish or other aquatic animals. Research in Sweden has shown that red-throated divers are unable to bring back enough fish to satisfy their young when foraging in acidified lakes.

The Flow Country streams are the home of the dipper and, as in other parts of highland Britain, the dipper is in difficulty, with its numbers dwindling on many waters. Research by the RSPB in mid-Wales has shown that dippers disappear from rivers when there is a shortage of food: there is a direct correlation between the numbers of dippers on a stretch of river and

The violation of the Flow Country

the numbers of caddis fly larvae. (Caddis larvae are not the only item in the diet of dippers but they are easy for a scientist to collect and estimate their abundance.) In some rivers the caddis and other invertebrate life have gone so the water is effectively dead.

There is a nice (if that is the correct word) illustration of the effect of acid rain and afforestation on the aquatic environment around the RSPB's reserve at Gwenffrwyd, 3 kilometres from Dinas where we had been to see the kites. Afon Gwenffrwyd runs out of hills dominated by conifer plantations and it has lost its otters, the predators at the top of the river food chain, but their signs are still common on a tributary, the Melyn, which runs out of mainly open ground where acidification is minimal.

The second point that attracts my concern about afforestation of the Flow Country has made it a hot potato for reasons more contentious than a straightforward 'development versus wildlife' conservation debate. The opinion of Roy Dennis, the Highlands Officer for the RSPB, was given to us without pulling any punches. 'We, as conservationists, may have to accept that things might have to happen in some very special places if the good of the nation is overriding, but when the crop of trees is in the long run not as valuable as people say – that it has tremendous problems with windthrow and insect pests and so on, and the reason for planting was not to do with true forestry but for tax-relief and profit from changes in land value – that's a double kick in the stomach'. The economics of forestry cannot be kept in isolation and losses in the game, fishing, sheep and deer industries of a remote community, especially in terms of local employment, must be set against any benefit from forestry.

We also spoke to Roger Cadwallader, forester for Fountain Forestry, who was convinced that forestry was a patriotic necessity. His view is that Britain needs to grow trees to reduce expensive imports and the trees he is planting will be of real benefit. He made the point that, to be properly effective, a complete forestry system is needed. It must have an area large enough for a rotation of planting and felling to provide material for sawmills and pulp factories on a continuous and sustainable basis. This would require a further 40,000 hectares planted in the Flow Country to bring the total to the Government's recommended 100,000 hectares for a viable industry.

Roger pointed out that people complain about 'blanket afforestation' but there are, to use his phrase, 'blanket SSSIs' – 27,000 hectares in Strath Halladale alone. There would then still be, he claimed, 'plenty of space for birds'. Wildlife needs space for viable ecosystems with sustainable breeding populations, as much as forests need viable plantations but, unfortunately, SSSIs are not inviolable protected areas.

It cannot be disputed that, if afforestation is to be done, then it should be done well, but is Roger's optimism about the co-existence of plantations and wildlife justified? I would like to think that this leaves room for substantial stretches of untouched countryside and populations of birds so I put the question to a botanist and an ornithologist with considerable experience of the flows.

Dr Richard Lindsay of the Nature Conservancy Council described the effect of even small forest blocks in a treeless scene. The foliage intercepts the rain, which evaporates from the needles, and roots suck water out of the ground so that trees effectively reduce rainfall by nearly half. Coupled with the increased drainage, the result is a progressive leakage and drying out of the surrounding bog. This is happening piecemeal all over the Flow Country so the destruction is far greater than the area of plantation would suggest.

Dr Des Thompson, also of the Nature Conservancy Council, echoed this view. Waders cannot simply move out and settle again in front of the advancing trees. They are finely tuned to their habitats and each individual bird needs an intimate knowledge of its immediate habitat to find food and shelter and avoid predators. When birds are forced to quit their homes this special relationship collapses. Some will die and others will attempt to settle on second class ground or have to compete with neighbours. Too much fragmentation will exaggerate these problems and it is possible that some areas bordering plantations will become devoid of waders.

We live in an overcrowded island where both individuals and the nation must earn a living, so we should expect such a large area, especially in a depressed region, to try to earn its keep. The communities in the Flow Country are facing very hard times, with dwindling school registers as clear evidence, but is forestry the solution? There is a very real problem of what to do with the northern fringes of Scotland. It has always been an underdeveloped area

Dippers are sensitive to the effects of forestry around their river habitat

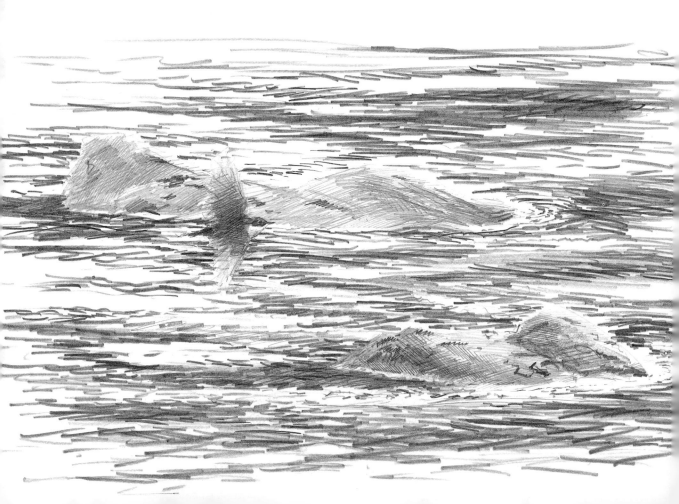

and two centuries ago, the infamous Highland Clearances was a heavy-handed (to say the least) attempt to deal with overpopulation and poverty. The sheep and sport based economy that replaced the old system after the Clearances is becoming less viable but, wildlife conservation apart, it is difficult to see that forestry is the answer. We did not have time to talk to many local people but we were told that forestry has not benefited the local population because most of the work is done by outside contractors. Meanwhile the local community has to foot the bill for strengthening roads which were not designed to take heavy machinery and eventually timber lorries. In the south-west of Scotland where large stretches of country have been forested, whole communities have withered. There is no employment to be had while the trees are growing.

Whatever is done to help the inhabitants of the Flow Country will require huge investment in one form or another. It seems a pity that so much public money was spent with so little deliberation. Ultimately, however, the tragedy of the Flow Country is that it took 10,000 years to create and the current changes are irreversible. Bruce recalled a saying that 'art is not painting what you see, but painting what you want to make others see'. Writers do the same with their words; it is impossible to do otherwise. If you hear someone say 'Let's face the facts...', you can be sure you will be treated to a selection of facts (and interpretations masquerading as facts) that support their argument. In discussions on the afforestation of the Flow Country, I have found that the conservationists have been most successful in producing the facts that make me see what they want me to see. But, of course, I want to see greenshanks, dunlin and divers in a squelchy, green wilderness.

FOUR

WINGED ASSASSINS

BLACK ROCK lies at the end of one of the more extreme examples of a Cornish lane. The metalled road is just one car width wide and so closely hemmed in by high banks that passing another car is a major manoeuvre. The lane winds round tight corners, drops into a deep valley or coombe and then climbs out again to some field gates where we found just enough space to park.

A narrower lane took us to the cliffs. It was almost a tunnel because its banks were topped by hedges of hawthorn, still in blossom, that had grown lopsided in the Atlantic gales until the lee side formed a roof. Memories of a postwar West Country childhood, when cars were few and slow and road maintenance sparing, were evoked by the profusion of wayside flowers. The green banks were washed with the pinks of foxglove and blocks of red campion, while eyebright and pansy peeped out from the grasses. Wall pennywort with its round, button leaves and spikes of white flowers was unfamiliar to eastern eyes, so was the common lizard that scuttled across in front of us. And there were plenty of butterflies – whites, meadow browns, speckled woods and red admirals.

From the end of the tunnel, we skirted a field, rounded a corner and found ourselves on the edge of a cliff with the sea swishing around the rocks 500 feet below us. What a dramatic landscape it was. Across a deep cove we were looking at the sheer wall of Black Rock and beyond it, running into the distance, the ragged coastline of north Cornwall. As the relentless sea has torn and picked into the rock over millions of years, it has opened bays between outcrops of harder rocks and left behind stacks and pinnacles standing out of the water. Even in the calm weather that blessed our visit, the seascape was more dramatic than anything that we had seen in the landscapes of Wales and Scotland.

This story is different from our others partly because the landscape consists of a narrow strip, often less than a stone's throw across, from the bordering wall or fence at the top of the cliff to the tide's edge at the bottom. It is also different because our key bird, the peregrine, occupies such a large part of the story. As with the unrivalled Cornish cliffs, no other bird we saw on our travels could match the magnificence of the peregrine. We were also lucky because we were accompanied by Dick Treleaven who has devoted over 40

Black Rock lies on the Atlantic coast of North Cornwall

years to the peregrines of north Cornwall. He has watched them in all seasons, painted them, written about them and enthused over them, freely imparting his hard-won knowledge to anyone who shows an interest in his passion.

Compared with the cliffs bordering other stretches of the British coastline, the Cornish cliffs are comparatively empty. There were no massed colonies of seabirds; the puffins that once burrowed into the tops have disappeared although the guillemots have increased on the ledges. The peregrines, however, are there for anyone to see and they make one of the nation's most exciting bird spectacles, but our enjoyment was heightened hugely by Dick's commentaries on their behaviour. Nevertheless, this story is not only about peregrines. The Cornish cliffs, like those anywhere around the coastline of Britain, form an interesting habitat, at once related to but divorced from the

– 83 –

surrounding country. The drive by farmers to profit from every scrap of land has pushed the plough almost to the edge of many cliffs and barely left room in some places for a cliff-top path. On the remaining narrow strip and on the less precipitous slopes there survive a remnant of the flora and the associated bird life which once flourished inland, together with specialist cliff species. Typical cliff birds, such as ravens and jackdaws, fulmars and gulls also inhabit the cliffs. The cliffs are also a haven for badgers burrowing into the upper slopes and grey seals who bear their pups in sheltered caves at the bottom.

The Peregrine Falcon

No bird causes so much excitement as the peregrine falcon. People pay large sums to acquire rare parrots, shoot grouse or go on cruises to visit albatrosses on their nests, but never is there such universal enthusiasm as greets the sight of a peregrine stooping at its quarry, whether in the wild or flown from the falconer's wrist.

For over one thousand years the peregrine has been regarded as a noble bird. When hawking was the universal recreation for those with the time and money to indulge, the peregrine was the 'falcon gentle' with gentle meaning well-born as in Chaucer's 'parfait gentil knyght'. The esteem in which it was held is firmly based on the peregrine's skill as a hunter.

This is the bird we had come to watch. I had seen peregrines before in different parts of the world but they had always been glimpses of birds flying past or perched, distant and unapproachable, on high cliffs. They had been

Peregrines

enough to say that I had seen a peregrine. The Cornish cliffs give the peregrine a linear habitat. They hunt along the edge, and at this time of year rarely stray far from the eyrie, so we stood a good chance of excellent views of the aerial prowess that has given the peregrine its reputation.

Peregrines at Work

The day was fine but a stiff breeze prevented us from getting too comfortable as we settled down against a boulder with grandstand views of events at Black Rock. While getting our bearings and settling comfortably into our look-out we had already sighted the peregrines.

The eyrie was out of sight on a ledge where it would escape direct sun for most of the day, which meant that it was visible only from the sea. However, it was clear that the peregrines had found a place where the wind blowing up the cliff gave them the lift for hanging head to wind until they sighted a victim – 'waiting on' Dick called it. If they disappeared on some errand, we knew we would eventually spot them again at the same point.

The peregrines were immediately obvious among the gulls in the same area, first by their smaller size and then on closer examination by the characteristic shape and ability to hang motionless, as if at the end of a string, like a kite. I had thought that kestrels were masters of riding the wind but the pair sharing Black Rock with the peregrines were not able to match their skill.

While we waited for action we could concentrate on examining the peregrines and their characteristic outline, 'like flying coathangers', someone said. The difference in size between the sexes was striking. The male was noticeably smaller, hence its falconers' name of tiercel which is derived from the Latin *tertius* – one third, although it is one third *less* than the female's weight rather than one third *of* it. Shakespeare's Juliet equates Romeo with a male peregrine when she appeals

O, for a falconer's voice,
To lure this tassel-gentle back again!

The female is simply 'the falcon' because this was the sex favoured by falconers as she could deal with larger quarry such as herons. As a result the name became applied to the species as a whole. We use the female 'goose', 'duck' and often 'cow' as collective names for animals of both sexes in much the same way.

While waiting on, the peregrines occasionally trampolined – dropping earthwards and soaring vertically back up without a wingbeat. Perhaps they were relieving the tedium of their watch, like a sentry marching up and down in front of his box; it certainly gave us something to watch. Suddenly the falcon started flapping, moving very slowly forward. 'She's lining up' said Dick. Then the wings began to bite the air and the falcon surged forward. 'She's

A peregrine's stoop, miss and final kill

away' cried Dick. It took all my concentration to follow just one peregrine as it folded its wings and tipped into a headlong stoop. I could track it through binoculars only because the sun highlighted its body so it shone against the dark, shadowed cliff behind it.

Out of the corner of my eye, beyond the rim of the binoculars' eyepiece, I glimpsed a flock of three or four pigeons coming in from behind us, flying low around the head of the cove and heading for the peregrines. The tiercel attacked first, turning over and swooping up at one pigeon. It missed, broke off, 'throwing up' to gain height and stooped again. The pigeon avoided it and a desperate chase started. The pigeon flew up the slope and over the top of the cliff, hugging the ground and dodging to left and right with the tiercel in hot pursuit. It might have got away but the falcon came winging in from the side and struck, binding to the pigeon in a cloud of feathers and dropping out of sight. All that remained of the encounter was a single pigeon feather blowing across the cove.

It was only after the sky had cleared of birds that we could get our breath back, compare notes and hear Dick's comments. It had been an impressively powerful image. One moment the peregrines were hanging on the wind, and then they were off, powering through the air, and into the sizzling dogfight. I could not help cheering on the pigeon; it was clearly the underdog. The outcome of the chase was only one meal for the peregrines but it was life for the pigeon. I have not witnessed anything so strongly emotional since watching killer whales hunting seals. Watching lions or cheetahs stalking and plunging after antelopes on a television screen cannot convey the same sense of drama.

Cooperative hunting by a pair of peregrines is not unusual. Dick says the lighter tiercel soars higher and, when they hunt together, he sets off first. He can climb quicker with his better weight to wing area ratio, but the powerful female flies faster. Pigeons can be spotted when they are still two miles distant. This gives the peregrines time to get into position above them. If the wind is offshore they may have to beat inland to gain height so, if they have not had enough warning, they may see the pigeons fly past without being able to give chase. Dick has watched peregrines fail to make a kill all day, then the wind has changed in their favour and they have made several quick kills.

Early warning was not necessary today, with flight after flight of pigeons coming along the coast like targets in a shooting gallery. The pigeons do not like going over open water so they have to run the gauntlet of the waiting peregrines. Unlike many other birds of prey, peregrines do not like to move far from the eyrie and they wait for their food come to them. Even so, the outcome is not certain and we saw more failures than successes.

Presumably the sport of falconry would have lost its appeal if the outcome of flying a falcon at its quarry became monotonously predictable. It would have been no more sport than shooting sitting ducks. Two things prevent this. In level flight there is probably not much speed difference between a peregrine and a pigeon. Moreover the pigeon is more manoeuvrable. The peregrine has, therefore, to gain height so that it can accelerate in a dive, but it must not go too fast or it will not be able to follow the pigeon's dodges. Fine control of flight is essential because there is a difference measured in millimetres between missing a kill and colliding with the victim so hard that the peregrine's own safety is imperilled.

The results of hunts are tipped in favour of the peregrine getting ample meals. In a bout of serious hunting, a pair will kill more than it needs. The surplus is cached and doled out during the remainder of the day. Once they have enough food, the peregrines lose interest. They will cease hunting altogether or merely chase victims half-heartedly, which makes them look pretty useless hunters and distorts calculations of their kill rate.

Now that we had followed one kill and knew what to expect, we could watch the next more carefully. Dick talked us through what the peregrines were doing, or what they were about to do. 'Not interested', I said as the falcon started to fly away from the flight line of the pigeons. 'Yes, she is', said Dick, and she soon turned about and went in a shallow stoop. I had been mistaken because the falcon was concentrating on making height rather than immediately chasing the pigeons. They would have escaped from a level chase. This is the problem when the wind is in the wrong direction: the peregrines cannot get into position quick enough and the pigeons slip past.

These pigeons bunched together and flew around the wall of the cove and tried to escape to seaward. Three times the peregrine attacked and missed. She would stoop and turn upside down to try to grapple with the pigeon from underneath. A glancing blow was no use as a pigeon forced down into the sea was as good as lost. The fight continued out of sight and we never saw the outcome but the falcon must have been successful because she did not come back into sight. She must have killed and plucked the pigeon somewhere round the corner.

The chase (opposite) and the strike (below)

Peregrine Biology

To the non-ornithologist, the naming of birds of prey is a little perplexing. What exactly are birds of prey and what is difference between a hawk and a falcon? The confusion stems from the arcane language of the ancient sport of falconry, which is also known as hawking. As in most sports, its practitioners have evolved their own language, and woe betide the outsider who gets it wrong! For present purposes, birds-of-prey, or raptors, are day-flying hunters (so the owls are out) which fall into two categories: the falcons and the hawks and eagles. The falcons include the peregrine, gyrfalcon, kestrel and merlin and are recognised by pointed wings – falconers call them 'long-wings'. The hawks, which have rounded wings, include goshawk and sparrowhawk – called 'short-wings' and the buzzard and eagles – called 'broad-wings'.

The peregrine gets its name from the same root as 'peregrinate' and it was once called the passenger falcon because of its migratory, wandering habits. This is reflected in its name in other languages: *pilgrimsfalk* in Swedish, *Wandervalke* in German and *faucon pèlerin* in French. In the lowland counties of

A peregrine watching and waiting in the early morning

Britain, the peregrine has always been a winter visitor and peregrines take up residence especially in estuaries and reservoirs where they can be certain of feeding well among the winter flocks of waders and wildfowl. The Hundred Foot Washes is often a good place for spotting a peregrine, and so, I gather, is St Paul's Cathedral where starlings are plentiful. When there is a stampede of birds into the air, look around for the peregrine!

Migration is stimulated by a failure of the food supply in the nesting area. The Cornish peregrines with their year-round supply of pigeons tend to stay on the cliffs whereas, as the peregrine authority Derek Ratcliffe points out, the population on the west coast of the Scottish Highlands is more mobile. They depend on seabird colonies and when the inhabitants depart for the open sea in late summer, the peregrines are forced to move. There are no large estuaries locally to provide an alternative diet and the moors are comparatively barren. Dick has found that it takes bad weather to drive his Cornish peregrines away from their cliffs and then they merely fly inland to catch farm pigeons. He has a regular New Year's Day peregrine watch at Black Rock, fortified by flasks of mulligatawny soup.

The advantage for any bird staying on its nesting ground all winter is that it can start breeding as early in the year as possible and there is no danger of its territory being been usurped in its absence. The pattern for many resident birds is to start courting in autumn, then to lose interest through the winter and recommence in spring. This is seen in many familiar birds and is at its most obvious with rooks and mallards. It is also the pattern of the Cornish peregrines but courtship really starts in March. Dick had drawn our attention to some half-hearted displays in which a tiercel stooped and soared, giving little flickers of wingbeats as an advertisement, probably to a passing peregrine that we had not seen. This must be a pale imitation of the show that is put on by tiercels when they are keen to attract the attention of a falcon at the start of the season.

The first stage is easily missed: the tiercel flies to and fro along the cliff

Seventeen day-old peregrine eyasses

Jackdaws sailing in an updraught

edge, calling to draw the attention of any passing falcon. When the two have become acquainted, they indulge in a riotous display of flying skills which include some of the most accomplished aerial evolutions in the bird world. They take turns to stoop at each other, climbing high and hurling themselves at their partners, often missing by inches, and using the momentum to lift them back to the starting height. As described earlier, it seems that peregrines hold back in their hunting stoops to retain control but this is unnecessary when courting. The bird is free to hurtle down and swing up without thought of safety. Although the bird may just miss its partner, this is as good as a mile when compared with the danger of striking a victim.

Enthralled as we were with the summer peregrines, we could tell what we have missed by not seeing them at courtship from Joseph Hagar's descriptions of a Massachusetts pair: 'again and again the tiercel started well to leeward and came along the cliff against the wind, diving, plunging, saw-toothing, rolling over and over, darting hither and yon like an autumn leaf until finally he would swoop up into the full current of air and be borne off on the gale to do it all over again....Nosing over suddenly, he flicked his wings rapidly 15 or 20 times and fell like a thunderbolt. Wings half closed now, he shot down past the north end of the cliff, described three successive vertical loop-the-loops across its face, turning completely upside down at the top of each loop, and roared out over our heads with the wind rushing through his wings like ripping canvas.' These whirlwind evolutions remind me of Mark Twain's description of a courtship display by another American male: Tom Sawyer showing off in front of Becky Thatcher. Presumably the objective is the same in the male of both species.

As the pair gain familiarity and confidence, they begin to hunt together, chasing the same victim, but later their behaviour changes again. The male hunts alone for food which he presents to the female either with an aerial transfer when she flies out to meet him or by handing it to her on a perching ledge. As the laying date approaches, the tiercel's provisioning of his mate becomes more important.

The usual clutch is three or four eggs and, judging by writers' effusive descriptions of their appearance, they mean more to a collector than simply adding another species to his hoard. Like other falcons, no nest is made to receive the eggs and they are incubated on the bare ledge by the female. She is fed by the male who only takes a shift on the eggs while his mate is feeding

A gliding raven

or on the rare occasions when she hunts for herself.

When we visited Cornwall the eggs had hatched and the well-grown young were left to their own devices on the ledge while both parents hunted. As the Black Rock eyrie was virtually invisible, Dick took us to another farther down the coast. The eyrie was just below the top of a sheer cliff at the back of a narrow cove, so we could crawl to the edge at the neck of the cove and, with the aid of our telescopes, watch without disturbing the birds; no doubt perplexing walkers on the cliff path that passed a few yards above the nest.

The downy nestlings were nothing special to look at. Like any young bird that is being reared in the nest rather than wandering around in search of its own food, they lack grace and their short lives are devoted to gorging with food and growing. Much more captivating was the falcon that perched close enough for a marvellous view without being greatly upset by our presence. However, we soon retreated and left Bruce at a safe distance to record the nursery scene on his sketchpad.

Much later he rejoined us, thoroughly excited. While busy recording details of the nestlings, the falcon had flown in with a pigeon, still dripping red. She paused only long enough to show it to the nestlings and then took it to a nearby ledge where she proceeded to pluck it. When the carcass had been cleaned the falcon brought it back and commenced to feed the nestlings. There was something touching in the contrast between the powerful action of the bill in ripping off chunks of flesh and the delicacy with which the falcon proffered the morsels to the nestlings. Each one was fed in turn and, as they became replete, the falcon swallowed more chunks herself and held out fewer to her brood and eventually she removed the carcass.

The nestlings are properly called eyasses, a name derived from the Norman French *niais* – a nestling, which became 'a nyas' and then 'an eyas or eyass'. To the falconer, any peregrine taken from the nest is an eyass to distinguish it from a 'passager' caught in its first year and an adult 'haggard'. The eyasses spend five or six weeks on the nest ledge. They start to hop from rock to rock and then are caught by the wind and find themselves airborne. It takes a few days for them to become proficient enough to take food from their parents in flight and they start hunting games and practising attacks on insects or even plants. Dick says that he has seen the adults catch and release pigeons so that the young peregrines can pursue them. He can also sometimes predict which ones are going to survive when the family ties are loosened in the autumn. Two thirds will die in their first year and the survivors are those that displayed the best hunting skills when they first took to the air.

Bouncing Back

When Dick Treleaven first became interested in the peregrine in the early post-war years, the British population was recovering from an

A peregrine plucking a kill

unprecedented attack. Keepering and the robbing of eggs and nestlings by egg collectors and falconers had had little effect on numbers during the first part of the century but in World War II *The Destruction of Peregrines Order* encouraged peregrines to be shot and their eggs destroyed to protect carrier pigeons which were used by submarine spotter-planes when maintaining radio silence. The slaughter was carried most zealously on the cliffs overlooking the Western Approaches and it left the eyries empty.

The recovery of the peregrine in the immediate post-war years was amazing. Legal protection was restored, keepering had declined and the species showed surprising resilience. Dick could not find a single occupied site in 1945 but they were recolonised from inland and 17 of the 20 known Cornish sites were reoccupied by 1954.

Then, mysteriously, the trend went into reverse. The 17 pairs dropped to

Pesticides caused egg-shell thinning, so many eggs were crushed during incubation

six, then to five, four, three, two and finally only one pair remained. Dick tried to promote a survey of peregrines to investigate this decline but failed. It was thought to be a local Cornish problem but, eventually, the pigeon fanciers, blaming a high population of peregrines for excessive losses among their racers, persuaded the government to make an enquiry into the status and habits of the British peregrine. The British Trust for Ornithology was commissioned to carry out the work and the results of a national survey showed that, far from an excess of peregrines as the fanciers claimed, 40 per cent of sites were unoccupied and only 20 per cent reared young. By 1962 the breeding rate had dropped to one-eighth and the population was heading towards extinction.

Dick was the first person to witness one of these inexplicable deaths. He saw a peregrine spin out of the sky like a top, completely out of control, and spent an hour searching for the bird. It was in tremors and died the next day.

The story of peregrines and pesticides has become a classic case-study in the annals of wildlife conservation and the war against environmental degradation. It has been set out in detail by Derek Ratcliffe in his book *The Peregrine Falcon*. Dr Ratcliffe is one of the band of ornithologists with a lifelong interest in the peregrine and was admirably suited to organise the BTO's enquiry. The search for a cause of the disaster soon focussed on poisoning.

During the 1950s there had been numerous reports of deaths among seed-eating birds, such as sparrows, finches and woodpigeons, which had been feeding on grain dressed with the powerful new insecticides aldrin, dieldrin and heptachlor. Chemical analysis of the bodies revealed these poisons in their tissues. There were also reports that predators were dying from eating the contaminated carcasses. The Cornish peregrines' diet of grain-eating pigeons would have immediately exposed them to pesticides. If, as suggested below, they choose to hunt obviously unfit birds, they would select pigeons which are already suffering from the poison. It is also possible that peregrines were suffering from the fanciers dusting their pigeons with pesticide powder to control parasites.

The next step in the detective work that linked the disappearance of peregrines with pesticides was Derek Ratcliffe's discovery of pesticides in addled peregrine eggs. It was also significant that the greatest losses occurred among peregrines living near arable farmland where they might be expected to prey on contaminated prey. There was a sideline to the pesticide story; Dr Ratcliffe had been puzzled by mysterious breakages of peregrine eggs in the nest. Comparing recent eggs with older specimens in collections showed that the thickness of the shell had begun to decrease since about 1947. This coincided with the widespread use of DDT and the involvement of this pesticide was later proved by analysis and experiment.

The overwhelming evidence of pesticide poisoning led to the partial banning of the most pernicious pesticides in 1962. There was an almost immediate drop in reports of wild bird deaths but peregrines did not respond for several years. However, they have now made a remarkable recovery, reappearing in many of their old haunts and recovering much of their pre-war range and numbers.

The recovery of the Cornish peregrines was a most exciting event for Dick Treleaven. The last attempt to breed in 1961 had been followed by a blank of nearly a decade. It must have been a depressing period but there remained one widowed falcon at Black Rock for him to watch. In June 1969, after he had noticed more kills around the eyrie than usual, he saw a newly fledged peregrine glide by. He never believed he would live to see the day that peregrines bred again on Cornish cliffs. Next year, four young were raised but successes were patchy until a dramatic recovery started ten years later.

There is now almost one new site occupied each year. The Cornish peregrines seem to be safe, but Dick refuses to confirm this. There are so many new chemicals coming into use and being liberated into the environment where they can work their way up the food chain that the guardians of the peregrines must maintain their watch. Moreover, there is the never-ending problem of disturbance and robbery. Increasing numbers of visitors flood into Cornwall, where they are encouraged to go into once untouched places, for instance being funnelled along the coast path above the remotest cliffs. Disturbance is unintentional but there are those whose visits to the cliffs are less welcome.

The Problem of Pigeons

Around the country, the main threats to peregrines are egg thieves and falconers, or more precisely, those who steal eyasses to sell to falconers, but Cornish peregrines are threatened more by the guns of pigeon fanciers. It is ironic that lovers of both peregrines and pigeons point to the survey that revealed the decline in peregrines as showing that they were instrumental in alerting the world to the dangers of persistent pesticides. And it is a reflection on human attitudes that pigeon lovers still blame the peregrine for exorbitant losses, although the survey that demonstrated the massive destruction of peregrine populations gave the lie to the fanciers' assertions.

No one can deny that peregrines eat racing pigeons. We had spent an exciting morning watching the gladiatorial contest as bands of racers ran the gauntlet of Black Rock. We were shown rings and flight feathers stamped with owners' names and addresses as additional evidence that these were birds that belonged to people who had spent money and time raising and training them.

As with the hen harrier that indisputably takes grouse chicks or the seal seen robbing salmon nets, it is not surprising that there is a call for direct action against the predator. I feel a certain sympathy for the pigeon fancier, keeper or fisherman, particularly the latter two who are making a living from animals but even for the former who may lose a pigeon worth hundreds of pounds. Are their actions so different from my onslaughts against woodworm and greenfly in house and garden?

There is, however, a matter of balance. Some people like pigeons and others like peregrines so, before the lives of rare wild birds are taken, the impact of peregrines on pigeons needs to be put into perspective. We talked to Dan Driscoll, a leading pigeon fancier from across the Bristol Channel. His attitude was that peregrines have an equal right to the sky. He pointed out that so many thousands of pigeons fail to return home each year that it would need an Air Force of peregrines to destroy them. Some pigeons get lost and

Peregrines and fulmars are often seen together on the Cornish cliffs

start a new life with their country cousins, the rock doves, or their town cousins, the street pigeons. Magnetic storms upset their navigation, they get caught in rain or contrary winds and die of exposure and they have all sorts of accidents. It would be as logical to ban television aerials or high-sided vehicles as to shoot all the peregrines.

One question that arose in discussion was whether peregrines, and other predators, select easily caught prey and are therefore killing animals which are doomed anyway. There is some evidence that there is at least a tendency for peregrines to take weak birds or ones of an unusual colour. An oft-quoted example is that of a German falconer who examined the bodies of rooks killed by a trained peregrine and an equal number which had been shot at random. Twice as many of the rooks taken by the peregrine were not in peak condition, through injury or being in moult. Dick Treleaven also considers that both quarry and peregrine recognise when a chase would be

A fulmar on a cliff ledge

unsuccessful. He has seen peregrines ignore pigeons flying within easy range and believes that the 'attitude' of the pigeon shows it has spotted the peregrine and is ready for an instant getaway. The peregrine knows that the pigeon knows and does not make the effort to pursue it.

Birds of the Cliffs

The peregrines became inactive during the afternoon but this did not worry me unduly. We had seen more than enough to make the visit a huge success and I was glad to have a respite to absorb and order the images of the peregrines in my mind. I have always envied writers who have the facility of give such rich and vivid eye-witness accounts as that of Joseph Hager. The only way is to play the memory of the incident through my mind's eye and try to match words to describe it.

It was also a chance to turn my attention to something completely different.

There was plenty of birdlife on the cliffs without the peregrines. I find the ka-leidoscope of birds passing along a cliff face endlessly fascinating. It takes only a slight breeze wafting up the cliff to support a bird in the air without it having to flap its wings. Bearing in mind that powered flight is the most stre-nuous exercise in the animal kingdom and that a gull, for instance, increases energy consumption by 15 times when it is flapping in straight and level flight. Any saving in fuel consumption is at a premium and one trick fre-quently employed by birds is to free-wheel by catching updraughts on their outstretched wings and soar with the minimum of effort.

We had already seen how peregrines have perfected the art of not only hanging motionless on the breeze blowing up the cliff but also changing posi-tion by imperceptible movements of their wings. Almost every other bird on the cliffs was using the same technique to the best of its ability. We were mildly surprised to hear pheasants calling among the bracken and gorse but amazed to see them gliding along the cliff edge. Pheasants are reluctant fliers. Their deep breast muscles and short, fingered wings power them almost vertically into the air but they soon switch to a glide with further bursts of flapping to keep airborne. These pheasants were gliding long distances by hugging the edge of the cliff.

Even heavy-bodied, short-winged cormorants were soaring along the cliff. It was, therefore, not surprising that swallows and house martins were hawk-ing for insects by sweeping to and fro. Meadow pipits and skylarks, too, were using the breeze to maintain their towering song-flights without the need to beat their wings. I saw one skylark drifting backwards while he sang in a strong breeze.

The cliff face was dotted with still, white shapes. These were fulmars and herring gulls sitting on their nests. Even with binoculars it was difficult to dis-tinguish them. At a distance both are white birds with grey backs and yellow bills. The difference is clear as soon as they take leave the nest. The flight of fulmars is stiff compared with gulls. Their wings beat like oars whereas those of gulls are flexible, rubbery almost by comparison. However, the fulmars are the masters of soaring on updraughts.

At times, there was a procession of gulls along the cliff. Some were drifting one way, some the other. Whether this was one movement between feeding ground and nests or two separate contrary flows I was never able to ascertain. If there is anything like a good breeze the fulmars sail to and fro and rise and fall without a wing-beat. Unoccupied birds seem to spend their time visiting other fulmars on the cliff, paying special attention to those that are squatting on a ledge but not nesting.

As they pause on the wind, the fulmars drop their legs and raise their tails to act as airbrakes and help balance their movements. While they are hover-ing, the small changes to the set of wings and tail can be seen. They are finely detailed and as continuous as the trimming of the sails by a yachtsman to

Cliff habitat
– coast of North Cornwall
May /26/90.

Devilsbit scabious, thrift and reindeer moss can all be found growing on the cliff edge

extract the best from the last breath of wind and outpace his opponents.

There was no such finesse about the jackdaws and ravens that inhabited the slopes behind the cliffs. The jackdaws were nesting in a rocky outcrop and were busy bearing beakfuls of food to their nestlings. The wind was helping to ease the hard work of filling gaping mouths but feeding the family is a serious business and there was none of the lightheartedness so often associated with jackdaws.

This is the most strenuous time of the year for any bird but the ravens had finished nesting already and their young were in the air. The family party that came past Black Rock at intervals throughout the day was lighthearted as they mixed tumbling displays with straightforward wind-assisted soaring. Ravens are one of my favourites. They may be traditional birds of ill omen but I have always found their conversation of croaks and squawks rather charming and they bring a little cheer to otherwise bleak scenery.

There was one cliff-top bird that was conspicuously absent from these cliffs. The chough is often called the 'Cornish' chough but it now no more a Cornish bird than the Manx shearwater is an inhabitant of the Isle of Man. Once occurring around the coast from eastern Scotland to the white cliffs of Sussex, the British population of some 300 breeding pairs is now confined to cliffs of western Wales and Scotland, with only a few pairs dispersed inland.

The loss of the choughs from the south-west, the last pair disappearing in 1967, is a great shame. They are charming birds; their broad wings make them even more adept at playing in the wind than their corvid relatives and the cliffs ring to their loud, twanging calls (their name ought to be pronounced 'chow' to imitate their voice). A widespread belief is that they have been pushed out of feeding grounds and nest sites by the jackdaw, but the preferences of food and nesting place differ in the two species. The main

Fulmars often hang in updraughts

decline took place in the 19th century when the choughs were hard-hit by long, cold winters, and egg-collectors then hastened their demise.

Choughs are fussier feeders than other crows, rarely scavenging for carrion or scraps, and they subsist primarily on insects, particularly leatherjackets, earthworms and other animals which they find by probing, curlew-like, into soil or animal dung. Hard winters hit choughs because frost sends soil invertebrates deep, beyond the reach of their long bills. Short turf is also necessary and the long-term decline and extinction of the Cornish chough seems to have been largely due to the disappearance of sheep-cropped pasture.

Operation Chough is a project whose aim is to resurrect the Cornish chough by liberating captive-bred birds at sites that, with a little management, will support free-living populations. I hope that this is successful because it would

Although choughs are no longer found in Cornwall, the cliffs are still home to their bigger cousins the ravens

Raven wind hanging down hillside.

be marvellous to see choughs flying again over the English countryside.

Comparing the recent history of peregrines and choughs in Cornwall demonstrates shows vital role of habitat protection in wildlife conservation. The peregrines bounced back once the threat to their individual survival – accumulating pesticides – had been removed. For choughs, there has been no natural revival and even an assisted return may founder because the landscape that underpins their survival has been destroyed.

FIVE

THE EMBATTLED HEATH

THE ROAD was quite open to the heath on each side, and bisected that vast dark surface like the parting line of a head of black hair, diminishing and bending away on the furthest horizon.' You cannot write about the Dorset heaths without quoting Thomas Hardy. The great sweep of heathland which he called Egdon Heath has been immortalised in his Wessex novels as a region with a distinctive character, a 'great inviolate place (that) had an ancient permanence'. To Hardy, 'the sea changed, the fields changed, the rivers, the villages, and the people changed, yet Egdon remained'.

If you choose the right spot on the Old Coach Road across Canford Heath, in the middle of the area Hardy called Egdon Heath, you may still be able to find a scene such as he described: the road quite open to the heath on each side and (just about) diminishing to the furthest horizon. I tried this when wandering over Canford Heath with Bruce in search of places to set up his easel. This was scenically perhaps the most exquisite of our six landscapes and inhabited by some animals and plants which I was particularly keen to find. Our pleasure was rather dimmed by the sharp realisation that Egdon was by no means inviolate. When Hardy was writing, about a century ago, Dorset heaths covered over 55,000 acres; now there are no more than about 4,000 acres, mainly in small fragments. Canford Heath is one of the largest fragments but its integrity as a heathland habitat is severely threatened.

The heathlands of southern England are a very special, but rather odd, habitat because they contain relatively few species yet are marvellous for wildlife. The paradox is resolved with the realisation that they are the home for many species that are rare or absent from other parts of the country. This is the place to find the Dartford warbler, the smooth snake, the turf ant and Dorset heath (a species of heather), all of which are typical of warmer habitats in southern Europe. The presence of these southern forms, especially the reptiles and insects, is partly due to the warmth of the sandy ground, compared with the shaded, richer soils in neighbouring localities.

The sandy soils of heathland are thin and acidic, and the vegetation that grows on them is sparse and rather monotonous, so they do not support a

OPPOSITE A view across Canford Heath

large insect fauna, neither do they bear a good crop of seeds. This, in turn contributes to the limited variety of birds. When Colin Bibby of the RSPB surveyed the birds of Hartland Moor, he found that birds were scarce on the heath – meadow pipit, wren and stonechat being the commonest species. Yet heaths attract birdwatchers to observe such special birds as Dartford warbler, nightjar, hobby and woodlark, while sand lizards and smooth snakes bring herpetologists, and entomologists will look for some notable insects: the speckled footman, bagworm and velvet ant (actually a wasp), the spider-hunting wasps, the oil beetle and the silver-studded blue butterfly.

It is the restricted distribution, or outright rarity, of many of species that makes heathland so attractive to naturalists but, for anyone who has an eye for the countryside and gets pleasure from steeping in the scenery, heathland is a pure joy. It is an uncluttered landscape of basic earthy hues. In painting terms, it is mostly raw and burnt siennas and umbers, with a mix of brown madder and some cobalt blue splashed into the shadows, overlaid with dots of crimson where the heather is coming into flower and slabs of cadmium yellow to highlight the gorse.

> *Ye commons left free in the rude rags of nature,*
> *Ye brown heaths beclothed in furze as ye be,*
> *My wild eye in rapture adores every feature,*
> *Ye are as dear as this heart in my bosom to me.*
> JOHN CLARE

But, if you want to adore these heaths, go there soon. In Dorset, and elsewhere, they have been disappearing. Bruce and I came to Canford Heath in high summer with the main object of finding three special heathland birds; nightjar, Dartford warbler and hobby.

Nightjar

Bruce decided to start work at dusk. As he said, there is a special magic about the heath at this time, when the heath scenery is reduced to a simple, smooth-shouldered landscape broken only by the sharp and lonely silhouettes of gorse and pine. My feelings were less poetic. I was suffering from the abominably hot weather in late July. Heathland seems to be a natural sun-trap, more so than other open country perhaps because of the dry sandy soil and the crisp, short shrubby vegetation that is so reminiscent of the garrigue and maquis in southern France. There was no way of escaping the heat in the middle of Canford Heath, but the evening brought welcome respite. Bruce had brought me here because, to quote Thomas Hardy once more, 'When other things sink brooding to sleep, the heath appeared to wake and listen'.

And what it would have heard is the song of the nightjar, the strange rattling purr that gave rise to the nightjar's old country names of spinner, wheelbird and churn-owl. The sound is unmistakable; a bit like the grasshopper warbler but much louder and, when heard in the distance, it takes on the quality of wood being sharply and very rapidly tapped with a mallet. There is also a directionless quality which adds to the eerie atmosphere imparted to the twilight world as first one nightjar, then another, starts up and sings for five minutes or more without a break.

> Lone on the fir-branch, his rattle-notes unvaried,
> Brooding o'er the gloom, spins the brown eve-jar.

Nightjars are more easily heard than seen but they can be found at twilight or on moonlit nights. The best time to see them is on a fine summer's evening, just as the light is fading and the moths are starting to fly about. The nightjars are only visible against the pale dome of the sky, so lie down to get the best field of view.

As so often when you travel a long way to see something special we thought we were going to be out of luck, but Stephen Lyman-Dixon, the warden of Canford Heath, introduced us to a new trick. He put a hand in his pocket and flicked out his handkerchief. Immediately a shadowy, long-winged shape came out of the gloom and circled around us. The male nightjar has a white patch on the tips of its wings and the corners of its tail which stand out distinctly in the dim light. The white flash of the handkerchief apparently fooled

The stiff bristles around a nightjar's mouth help funnel insects into
its enormous gap when feeding in flight

Nightjar chick.
— 8 days
Canford Heath
Dorset.

When eight days old nightjar chicks have well developed feathers, but still have some down

the nightjar into thinking that a rival male had intruded into his territory but nightjars sometimes hover around a human figure without any extra ruse. W.H. Hudson described nightjars coming to investigate his motionless figure and acting 'in the most fantastical manner – now wheeling round and round my head like huge moths, anon tossing themselves up and down like shuttle-cocks; in the meantime uttering their loud, rattling, castanet notes, and smiting their wings violently over their backs, producing a sound like the crack of a whip-lash.' The hankie trick had not been necessary anyway because we later watched the nightjar hunting for insects in the glow from the lights of Poole.

There was no chance of confusing a nightjar with an owl because of the characteristic long tail. The nightjar was flying close to the heather, quartering the ground rather like a harrier. In the same way that we had kept low to spot it against the sky, the nightjar may have been flying near the ground to get a better view of insects moving above it. The large eyes of the nightjar are adapted for detecting the contrast of shadowy prey against a pale background. The extra man-made illumination from the conurbation creeping up on the heathland may be an unexpected asset if it helps the nightjars spot their prey.

Next morning, Stephen brought us back to see nightjars in their daytime role. The plumage of mottled and streaked grey-brown is a perfect example of disruptive camouflage, and a nightjar is almost impossible to spot against any background, but especially among the varied browns of the heath. We were taken to an area where a fire had reduced a stand of young pine trees to white skeletons, twice head height. This is where you may expect to find nightjars perching if you search for an unexpected lump apparently growing on a bare branch.

We failed to find a perching nightjar but Stephen showed us a nest – no more than a plate-sized scrape in the dead brown litter under tall fresh bracken fronds, but so placed to give a good field of view and a clear line of escape. The female broods by day and she was sitting motionless in the so-called cigar posture, with her head lowered to make the outline of the body even less conspicuous. At a distance of four feet, she leaped off the nest and went into a distraction display, flapping her wings as if having a fit until she

Studies of nightjars

A hobby over the heathland skyline

disappeared into the bracken. No doubt this ruse would have prevented a predator noticing her well-concealed brood but we ignored her efforts and concentrated on the two well-grown nestlings.

They were as perfect in their camouflage as their mother and they remained motionless with their eyes almost closed. Large, bright eyes would attract attention so both adult and young nightjars rest with their eyes reduced to slits. This may also protect the eyes from bright light, in the same way that a cat's pupils are reduced to slits; perhaps both reasons are correct.

The warm summer of 1990 and the abundance of insects may lead to a good survival rate for young nightjars. They need all the help they can get because the species seems to be in decline. There was once a time when night-jars could be heard over much of the country where there was dry open land, with scattered trees and patches of bare ground. Heaths are ideal. The cause of the decline is thought to be a combination of the disappearance and frag-mentation of the heaths and other open country and the dwindling popula-tions of moths and beetles that nightjars feed on.

The Heathland Scene

Bruce was certainly right about the magic of sunset on the heath. As the light fades and the colours go, an air of tranquillity develops and time changes. This process of stepping back in time at sunset is something I have commonly felt in tranquil parts of the country but never so much as on the Dorset heaths. It is an antique landscape that is described most clearly in Hardy's *The Return of the Native* where the opening chapter and many of the subsequent scenes take place at night. What an empty, wild world it was! And what strange lives the inhabitants led: the reddleman stained red from the manufacture of dye for marking sheep.

It is the light that Hardy sheds on a way of life over 150 years ago that inter-ests me most in his novels. His characters seem to belong to an older age – I am surprised when they travel by rail – but life would not have changed much for the heathlanders over a couple of centuries. They were too remote from the changing world in the towns, but Hardy noted that change was be-ginning to take place, with 'intrusive strips and slices brought under the plough with varying degrees of success, or planted to woodland'.

English heathland is largely man-made. It covers ground that was once part of the primaeval wildwood and its characteristic plants and animals would have once lived in small colonies in natural clearings on cliffs and other places where trees could not take root. When the first farmers cleared the forest on dry, acidic soils, they made way for colonisation by heath and set the scene for a great civilisation. All around Canford Heath there are tumuli built on a foundation of heath and their greatest works, Badbury Rings, Maiden Castle and Stonehenge, are not far away.

For centuries the heathland landscape continued to be maintained by a hardly changing routine of grazing by sheep and ponies (Hardy's 'he'th crop-pers') and the gathering of turf and gorse for fuel. Without this activity the trees would have encroached and returned the land to forest, as they are doing on many heaths today. Agriculture was barely viable on the poor soils until the enclosures and new farming of the agrarian revolution that had such a profound effect in other parts of the country. Fragmentation of the heaths as they were won for agriculture started in the 18th century and the heaths that remain today are those that were so poor that they resisted even the new agriculture.

Heathland Plants

For all the glory of the heathland vista, it is the scene of an ecological disaster, albeit one that took place several thousand years ago. Through a combination of climatic change and human interference the tree cover on the heathland regions disappeared and was replaced by the heather vegetation. It is rather ironic that reversion to the original vegetation through invasion by trees is now viewed as a threat.

In the same way that a visit to the Flow Country invokes a discussion of the different meanings of bog, moor and moss (page 68), so a walk on a heath begs answers to questions about heath and heather. Once again, there is

A patch of burnt heather (top left), with new growth of gorse, and the three heathers: bell heather (top right), ling (bottom right) and cross-leaved heath (bottom left)

The vivid colours of gorse

conflict between regional variations and the generally imprecise use of common English words which is compounded by the scientists' redefinition to give precise meaning. A heath is almost the same as a moor in that it is open, uncultivated ground dominated by heather. Heath is derived from an ancient word for a wasteland that cannot be cultivated and is generally taken to mean a lowland habitat on sandy ground, while moors are highland and peaty areas. But ecologists call the whole lot heaths and refer to upland heaths for what the rest of us would probably call moors.

To say that heaths are dominated by heather is stating the obvious, especially when the plant family to which heather belongs is called the Heaths, as are some of the individual species! Heather is also called ling, a word of Norse origin, in northern parts of the country and, confusingly, sometimes called heath in southern counties. It is the most abundant plant on the lowland heaths, producing the magnificent sward of purple in late summer. Mixed with the heather there will be bell heather, also called bell ling or black heath, which prefers drier ground, starts to flower earlier than heather and has leaves in whorls rather than opposite pairs. Cross-leaved heath, also called bog heath or bell heath, grows on wetter ground. It is easily identified as its leaves form four distinctive rows along the stem. Dorset heath is a rarity but rhododendron, which rather surprisingly is a member of the heath family, is an invasive introduced weed. I discovered the full extent of the confusing range of common names of the heaths, of which the above is a small sample, in Geoffrey Grigson's *An Englishman's Flora*. This is a treasure trove of plant miscellany and contains a clear indication why botanists use scientific names: not to blind laypeople with their erudition but to make it clear precisely which plants they are talking about.

Heather can form a vigorous sward on large areas of open ground because it thrives on sandy, acidic soils which prevent the growth of more vigorous plants that take over on richer soils. It is helped by its slow growth which reduces the demand for nutrients and by fungi that live in its roots and assist the uptake of nutrients. A heather plant lives for about 40 years. It starts as a single stem like a tiny Christmas tree then becomes bushy as lateral stems overtake the original leader. The bushy, mature phase lasts from about 15 years to 25 years, when the stems start to collapse outwards. Bare soil is revealed between the old stems and dormant seeds are stimulated to germinate and produce the next generation. This would produce a mosaic of different aged plants on the heath but the heather is usually affected by grazing and burning. Heather plants can cope well with cropping by sheep, ponies and rabbits because, as the long terminal stems are cut, shorter stems and buds nestling between them are stimulated to grow, and the plants become thicker, like a well-clipped hedge. Too much grazing sets them back because these second and third lines of growth cannot keep up. Similarly, when a fire sweeps across the heath, regeneration takes place from buds at the base of the rootstock.

Gorse and Broom

When Linnaeus, the Swedish botanist famous for inventing the modern system of classifying living things, visited Putney Heath in 1736, he was so overcome by the sight of gorse in flower that he fell on his knees and thanked God for its loveliness. At certain seasons heaths are ablaze with colour as thickets of gorse burst into flower. In spring, the common gorse, also known as furze or whin, creates blocks of yellow around the edges of the heather, especially on disturbed ground. In late summer it is the turn of the two small species of gorse which nestle among the heather. Dorset heaths are home to both species, but they are not easy to separate. When in flower, the distinction can be made by measuring the length of petals: over 12mm for western gorse and under 12mm for dwarf gorse. After flowering, the species can be separated by the length of the calyx, which remains on the plant: over 9.5mm for western gorse and under for dwarf gorse. Canford Heath is one of the few places where both species can be seen growing side by side.

The prickly nature of gorse – one remembers Winnie the Pooh falling into a gorse bush after his unsuccessful adventure with the bees – and its growth in thickets suggests a plant that is useful only for creating a stock-proof hedge. Far from it. Gorse was used as fodder for horses and sheep, as may be attested by the unnatural shapes of bushes where these animals habitually graze, and it was once the custom to plant gorse for this purpose and crush the evergreen foliage in 'whin-mills' for winter food. John Evelyn, writing in 1662, commented that 'in Hertfordshire, ...their thickets of Furzes...yield them more profit than a like quantity of the best wheat-land in England.' Gorse faggots were used as fuel, and not only by the poorer members of society because the fierce heat was excellent for firing brick kilns and bread ovens. Gorse also yielded a yellow dye and its ashes contain potash, once used

A male Dartford warbler singing

for manufacturing soap. It also had a use in the social life of the rural community. There is a scattering of flowers throughout the year, enough for an ardent lover to deny the country saying that when gorse is out of bloom kissing is out of fashion.

Gorse is a member of the pea family, as is broom, another common heathland shrub showy yellow flowers. Both are recognised as such by the characteristic pea flowers and seed-pods. One of the evocative sounds of a summer day on the heath is the ticking among the broom as pods twist and burst open in the heat to eject their seeds. Gorse and broom are important for the birds of the heath. They provide cover for roosting and nesting and their richer insect fauna supplies more food than is available in the surrounding heather or grass.

The value of broom to birds was recognised centuries ago when the growth of broom was encouraged by falconers to maintain populations of quarry

An adult hobby

birds for their birds to fly at. It is said that this is the reason for the Counts of Anjou choosing a sheath of broom as their badge, which led to their descendants, Kings of England from Henry II to Richard II, becoming surnamed Plantagenet from the Planta Genista or broom plant. Warwick the King-maker declared:

I'll plant Plantagenet, root him up who dares
Resolve thee, Richard; claim the English crown.

More Interesting Plants

The poor soils of heathland may have an impoverished flora but, among the swards of heather and thickets of gorse, there are some species worth looking for. In the drier parts there is heath spotted orchid, heath lobelia and heath bedstraw. Wetter hollows have more variety with marsh and bog orchids, aromatic bog myrtle or sweet gale, marsh gentian which thrives after fires and bog asphodel.

One of the most widespread plants to be found nestling among the heather, on upland moors as well as on heaths, is tormentil. Its single, regular four-petalled flower is not striking to the human eye but to a bee the plain yellow petals have a distinct bull's-eye. This is invisible to us because it reflects ultra-violet light. Insect eyes are sensitive to this part of the spectrum and the dark centre which the bee sees in the centre of the tormentil flower acts as a nectar guide, directing its probing tongue into the nectaries at the centre. Nectar guides which are visible to the human eye are a feature of many flowers. Another heathland example is eyebright. Its flowers are only about ¼ inch long but it is worth getting down on hands and knees with a handlens and examining the delicate pattern of purple and yellow which serves as a nectar guide within the white corolla tube.

Some heathland plants have unusual adaptations for obtaining extra nutrition to survive on poor heathland soils. Eyebright belongs to the figwort family Scrophulariaceae, some of whose species are partial parasites, as well as having showy flowers. Heathland representatives also include lousewort (in damper areas) and cow-wheat. They have green leaves, but their roots attach to the roots of other plants from which they steal nutrients and water, and cow-wheat cannot survive without this connection.

A more obvious parasite is dodder, a relative of bindweed, once common as a weed of arable farms and still found on heaths where it grows on heather or gorse. It is a total parasite, rootless and leafless, and unable to survive alone. The stem branches into a mass of reddish threads which grows over the host, almost smothering it and sometimes turning it brown. The threads put out growths, called haustoria, which penetrate the host's stems and tap its vascular tissues to suck up water and nutrients, so threatening its survival. This

strange habit was, I am surprised to find, well known three centuries ago. In *The Compleat Herbal of Physical Plants* of 1694, dodder is 'This fawning parasite, and ungrateful guest, (which) hugs the herb it hangs upon, with its long threads, and reddish twigs; and so closely embraces it, that at length it defrauds the hospitable herb of its nourishment, and destroys it by its treacherous embraces'.

Growing with the louseworts in the damp hollows of wet heaths, there will probably be some insect-eating sundews and butterworts, although the latter do not occur on Canford Heath. These plants supplement their meagre diet on poor soil by catching and digesting insects. It is not unusual to find tiny flies caught on the glistening leaves and even damselflies are sometimes trapped. The leaves are provided with glands that secrete a sticky substance to trap the insect, whose struggles only serve to get it further entangled, and enzymes that digest its body. Charles Darwin made some pioneering experiments on insectivorous plants and showed that 'feeding' a sundew with tiny morsels of meat caused it to secrete digestive juices and that a well-fed plant produced more seeds than one left to rely on nutrients from a poor soil.

The Hobby

The name hobby is thought to come from the Old French *hober*, meaning to move or stir. If so, it describes the effect this small falcon has on flocks of small birds, which race for the cover of trees at full tilt when a hobby appears. Its cruising flight is a rapid winnowing alternating with glides on extended wings but, with a barely perceptible change in tempo, it hurtles through the air after its quarry.

The hobby's claim to be a heathland bird has been weakened by the realisation that it is much more common on farmland than was once thought. It was believed to be mainly confined to the heaths and downs from Dorset and Wiltshire to Sussex and Surrey but its range is now known to stretch to South Wales and Lincolnshire. There has been a recent extension in range but somehow a large proportion of the breeding population had been overlooked. The oversight may have been due the hobby's superficial similarity to a kestrel. However, the hobby is the smaller bird but its wings are longer and the tail shorter so that it gives the impression of an outsize swift hurtling through the air.

We were taken to a nest in the tallest tree of a spinney of pines but there was not much to watch. The female was sitting on the eggs and the male waited nearby on a bare branch where it enjoyed a good all-round visibility. I had hoped to see him call the female off the nest and pass food to her but was

OPPOSITE Hobbies feeding in flight

balked by the pair disappearing behind the trees for the transfer of food.

I had more luck seeing the male hunting when I was lying on a warm bank in the sun to watch dragonflies flying around a boggy hollow. Suddenly, there was a flash of wings and the hobby sped past. I was too slow to see what happened but as the hobby slowed and gained height I could see it bring one foot forward to its beak and start dismembering one of the dragonflies I had been watching.

Luckily for the conservation of rare species, hobbies do not prey exclusively on dragonflies. Small birds, especially aerial species such as swallows, martins and skylarks, and large insects, such as dor beetles, cockchafers and moths, are easily plucked out of the air and usually eaten in flight.

With this diet, it is not surprising that the hobby is a migrant and that it inhabits southern counties where swallows, martins and large insects are

A male Dartford warbler protecting its territory

plentiful. It nests late in the season, which explains why there were eggs in the nest when we visited Canford Heath in late July. This timing lets the hobbies take advantage of the flush of young birds leaving the nest on which to feed their own young.

Dartford Warbler

Several birds have country names that attest to their choice of a home among gorse or furze. The linnet is the gorse thatcher, furze linnet or whin linnet in different parts of the country; the stonechat is furze hacker and gorse chat; the whinchat is also furze chat and gorse chat and even the hen harrier has been known as the furze kite or gorse harrier. But the gorse bird *par excellence* is the Dartford warbler, once known as the furze wren.

The Dartford warbler's main home is in the maquis and garrigue region of the western Mediterranean. English heathlands, which are the northern equivalent, form the limit of its range and the presence of the Dartford warbler draws attention to the similarity of these habitats better than any other species. It is the only one of our birds that is almost exclusively confined to heathland, where it nests mainly in the heather and gets much of its insect food from the gorse.

I have always found identifying warblers difficult. Except when they first arrive and the leaves are barely out on the trees, the skulking habits of many make them difficult to recognise. The Dartford warbler is no exception because it hides deep in gorse bushes. It is frequently depicted perched on the top of a bush and one is lulled into the belief that a visit to the heaths will reveal Dartford warblers perched obligingly on the gorse. In fact, the species offers good sport for birdwatchers because skill and perseverance, or good fortune, are required to get satisfactory views. More often, it is glimpsed as a dark figure slipping through a gorse thicket or undulating between bushes, its long tail hinting at its identity. The best time to see Dartford warblers is on a fine summer morning when the males are singing from the bushes and flying up in brief song-flights, or later when young are in the nest and the parents scold intruders with tails cocked.

The main interest of the Dartford warbler is that, unlike most of the warblers, it is a year-round resident, with only a few individuals migrating across the Channel and heading south. The Dartford warbler looks a feeble flier but crakes and rails, which normally fly with great reluctance, are long-haul migrants. However, the Dartford warbler has the wing shape of a bird adapted for short-hop flights through foliage. Its rounded wings, like those of the sedentary Cetti's warbler, contrast with the longer, pointed wings of sedge and willow warblers, which are more efficient for long distance flight.

The decision on whether to migrate or stay is sometimes finely balanced. Of two closely related and very similar heathland birds, the stonechat is either

resident or a short-distance migrant and the whinchat is a long-distance migrant that winters south of the Sahara. Whinchats avoid the decimation of severe European winters which result in a serious reduction of stonechat numbers. The stonechats benefit by starting to nest before the whinchats return. They lay three clutches in a season to the whinchats' two and raise twice as many young, so they rapidly recover from a cold winter. Both species flourish but vagaries of climate favour first one then the other.

The Dartford warbler survives the winter because of the nature of the heathland. The heather and gorse are evergreen; the gorse especially supports a much higher population of invertebrates throughout the year than, for instance, a deciduous wood and the heather forms a thick mat where the warblers can hide from the effects of all but the worst snow and frost. So the Dartford warbler has the same strategy as the stonechat. It suffers from the hardest winters but is capable of quick recovery. Before the hard winter of 1962-3 there were over 60 pairs of Dartford warblers on the Dorset heaths, but in the next summer there were four. Recovery was delayed by late snow in 1966, but the Dorset population had risen to 48 pairs by 1970 and 286 in 1974.

However, the failure of the Dartford warbler to survive fragmentation of heathland casts a shadow over the continued health of the British population. It once nested as far north as Shropshire and Staffordshire, and as far west as Cornwall and east as Suffolk and Kent. Dartford warblers lived on Hampstead Heath and were still found on the London commons before the war. Now, there are few to be found outside the Dorset heaths and the New Forest.

Lesser Life

If you looking for somewhere to sit and wait for hobbies or Dartford warblers choose, if you can, a spot either on bare ground or by one of the pools that lie in the hollows in the heath. Then you can while away the time by watching the insects. They are worth more than a casual glance, not so much because they are special heathland forms, but because they have some interesting, observable habits. If the sandy surface is pocked with tiny holes and craters, a sand wasp will soon appear, zig-zagging at low level as it scans the ground for a suitable site for a burrow. There are several different kinds of sand wasps, but the most striking is the black and red *Ammophila* sandwasp.

The female sandwasp digs a burrow by excavating with her jaws and carrying the sand away. Then she covers the entrance and disappears into the heather. A while later she staggers back with a large caterpillar which is

OPPOSITE A silver-studded blue butterfly

'A jewel in the sunlight'

dragged into the burrow. The unfortunate caterpillar is not dead, but has been paralysed by the wasp's sting. While in suspended animation it will be consumed by the grub that develops from egg that the sand wasp laid on it. Before the sandwasp leaves the combined mausoleum turned nursery, she disguises the entrance as carefully as an Ancient Egyptian sealing his pharaoh's tomb. She closes the hole and tamps the sand with her head, or with a pebble held in her jaws (a rare example of tool-using by an insect) and sweeps away any loose debris. Yet, so good is her memory of its location, she will occasionally return to check how her grub is getting on and, if necessary, supply it with another caterpillar.

The Dorset heaths are famous for dragonflies which gather at pools to mate and lay their eggs. Some are rare and all are dependent on the pools remaining undrained and unpolluted. While we were waiting for the hobbies to put in an appearance, we waited by a small pool which was being visited by a common darter, a small species which also frequents my Cambridgeshire garden pond, and the large and striking emperor dragonfly. The darters were courting, flying in tandem with the male clasping his mate by the scruff of her neck. He will maintain this hold until the business of egg-laying is finished, so that no other male may cuckold him. The female emperors were laying alone, pushing their abdomens deep into the waterlogged bogmoss. It is often possible to watch the large hawkers, like the emperor, hunting over the pool or on the open heath. Their large eyes detect the movements of other insects as much as 30ft away and they have stereoscopic vision for judging the range as they close at speed. All this makes watching a hawker dragonfly hunting flies as exciting as watching a hobby hunting dragonflies!

Of the butterflies, graylings fly up and then settle again on bare sand, where they are well camouflaged. After landing they turn until sideways on to the sun and then tilt their wings towards it. This may be to reduce their shadows or to trap heat from the sun and warm their bodies, or both. The silver-studded blue was the more conspicuous species in late July. It is a specialist heathland species and lays its eggs on heather and its relatives as well as on gorse and broom. The silver-studded blue's caterpillars enter into the same symbiotic relationship with ants as the ill-fated large blue butterfly. The caterpillars are carried into the ants' nest where they are sheltered and fed on ant larvae in return a sugary secretion, called honeydew, that the ants collect from the caterpillars back. The large blue became extinct in Britain because it was not appreciated in time that its conservation depended on preserving the rabbit-cropped grasslands that the host ants need. The silver-studded blue is becoming rarer as heathlands are lost, or not managed to conserve their ant hosts.

Heathland Management

'Though ..."to burn on any waste, between Candlemas and Midsummer, any grig (a Celtic word for heather), ling, heath, furze, goss (gorse) or fern (bracken), is punishable with whipping and confinement in the house of correction"; yet, in (Woolmer) Forest*, about March or April, according to the dryness of the season, such vast heath-fires are lighted up, that they often get to a masterless head...The plea for these burnings is, that, when the old coat of heath, etc. is consumed, young will sprout up, and afford much tender brouze for cattle; but, where there is large old furze, the fire,

---

* Despite its name, Woolmer Forest, in Gilbert White's time, consisted entirely 'of sand covered with heath and fern...without having one standing tree'.

following the roots, consumes the very ground; so that for hundreds of acres nothing is to be seen but smother and desolation,...and, the soil being quite exhausted, no traces of vegetation are to be found for years'. So wrote Gilbert White in his *Natural History of Selborne*. Fire is a double-edged weapon in heathland management, a blessing and a curse.

Fire has been a traditional method of maintaining the heather vegetation of heaths and moors. A fast-moving fire burns off the old growth without baking the ground so seeds and the buds on rootstocks survive and the burnt ground becomes revegetated. Animals that were driven out by the fire then spread back in to recolonise the area. Ideally, patches of ground should be burnt so that there is a rotation of heath at all stages of development, but the heaths now exist in fragments too small for burning to be used for management. But fires lit accidentally or through acts of vandalism now threaten their existence. In the dry summers of 1975 and 1976 over 10 per cent of Dorset heaths were burnt and Surrey fared much worse. Vandals burnt over 200 acres of Canford Heath last year.

The vegetation will eventually recover from burning and while touring Canford Heath I could see places where the vegetation showed signs of a rapid recovery after a fire. There was one patch of blackened ground, burnt in May last year but already studded with yellow plate-sized clumps of flowering gorse. The main danger is to the critical populations of rare animals. Individuals of less mobile species cannot escape the advancing flames; eggs and nestlings are particularly vulnerable. Fire may also remove critical blocks in the mosaic of habitat in small areas of heath; if the fires are frequent enough heather plants never attain the mature growth needed by Dartford warblers and smooth snakes. Another problem with fire is that it lets other plants invade and prevents the heather re-establishing itself. But this is another instance of fire being double-edged: judicious burning also prevent invasion and keeps the heather healthy.

The remaining patches of Dorset heaths are an object lesson in the importance of conservation by management. Without the traditional grazing and burning, heather degenerates and the heath is progressively invaded by birch, pine, bracken and increasingly rhododendron. Indeed, by deliberately neglecting management, unscrupulous owners can destroy the conservation importance of a heath and strengthen the case for a planning application. Management is, however, expensive and time- consuming. Pine saplings can be removed by cutting but birches and rhododendrons regrow from stumps so chemical treatment is needed. Spraying only partly controls bracken and may harm other species, so repeated cutting is needed to control it.

This is only part of the management story. The heathland animals have

OPPOSITE A male sand lizard

Housing development is encroaching on Canford Heath

precise requirements which will tax the ingenuity of a conservation manager with a range of species to preserve. There must be bare ground where lizards and snakes can bask and lay their eggs, and for wasps and bees to burrow. Wet hollows and pools are needed for dragonflies and bog plants. The birds, such as Dartford warblers, need some gorse, which must be managed to keep it as dense bushes, and birch saplings to provide food. On the other hand, nightjars need trees, or more specifically an edge between trees and open heath, for feeding. There is a fine balance to be struck because if the tree density maintaining the maximum number of nightjars is exceeded their numbers rapidly crash.

We saw some marvellous sights on Canford Heath: the hobbies and nightjars, Dartford warblers, dragonflies, butterflies and rare reptiles. The scenery alone made the visit worthwhile but my memories are suffused with sadness. Canford is beleaguered. Once the centre of Egdon Heath, it is struggling to survive.

The Welsh oakwoods, Norfolk pastures, and now the Flow Country are reduced to fragments while the East Anglian fens have all but disappeared. Each one has given way to intensive forms of land use, yet none is disappearing as fast or becoming so totally useless for wildlife in the face of human development as the Dorset heaths. Stephen Lyman-Dixon took me to a high point on the heath where we could see the sweep of heather but below us, looking towards Poole Harbour and distant Studland Heath was solid conurbation (you could not really describe it as a town because there was no heart). No more than six years ago, it was heathland all the way.

There were blocks of housing estate where houses were jammed cheek by jowl, supermarkets, light industrial complexes and recreation complexes. It was a total human environment with nothing left for anything else. It stopped at the heath: there was a wall with, on one side houses that were hardly vernacular in their design, and on the other side the heath with its smooth snakes and dragonflies. There was not the gentle transition into countryside that you get with a slowly, naturally expanding human settlement, except that the council had blurred the boundary by dumping hardcore on, and digging a drain in, a rather nice patch of wet heath that bordered the wall.

Stephen's employer is a property company that intends to transform Canford Heath into a nature reserve (it is already a Site of Special Scientific Interest or SSSI). Many of the inhabitants of the neighbouring conurbation treasure the heath and dearly want to preserve it but they are ranged against those whose attitude is, to say the least, negative. As I was about to take my leave, a column of black smoke spurted from the heath. 'Stolen car' said Stephen, and he was right. When we arrived it was well alight but we could see that the number plates had been removed. The flames were just creeping into the heather yet our efforts with fire brooms failed to check them. The fire brigade arrived some time later and quickly dowsed the flames but, if there had been more wind and the flames were fanning out over the heath, the firemen would have had a serious problem. The fire officer was vehement that a large heath fire would tie up the brigade so effectively that Poole and Bournemouth would be left without adequate cover for a dangerously long period.

The burning car set the seal on my feelings of pessimism but should I allow one incident to colour my conclusions on the future of heathlands? There are those who are determinedly optimistic. Martin Auld, the RSPB's heathland officer, sees a sea-change in the attitude towards heaths. Held in check by public opinion and the economic climate, building has slowed down and planning permission applications have almost dried up. There will still be losses and there are problems of encroaching trees and swarming people – walking, jogging, horse riding, motor cycling, mountain biking, vandalising – but the RSPB sees the possibility of turning a net loss of heathland into a gain with active management of the remaining fragments and even recreation of areas that have been lost.

It would be nice to be optimistic and be heartened by the new changes in the countryside – the slowing down of planting on the flows, making farm practices less intensive – and by the recovery of some wildlife species, such as peregrines and kites, but it is a rearguard action. If Canford Heath becomes a nature reserve, it will probably need a fence to keep people out, and what was a wilderness until a few years ago will be little more than a wildlife park. Perhaps that is the best we can expect, given the inexorable advance of our species.

Adder

SIX

NEAR NEIGHBOURS

THE DRIVE through the lanes of north Norfolk took us through some delightful scenery. It is not wild country, northerners may find it soft and effete, but it is the gentle English countryside where there are still places that could be inhabited by hares, squirrels and little grey rabbits and all the other childhood characters who dwell in a rural idyll. Winding lanes run between high hedges and wide verges, through tidy fields, over slow brooks and past small thickets and copses. They link villages of picturesque, flint and brick, pantile-roofed houses clustered around church and pub, and dominated by the gentry's halls. The names of the villages are Burnham Thorpe (Nelson's birthplace), Stanhoe, Tattersett, Docking, Great Walsingham and even Little Snoring. Just out of sight, there is the North Sea, beyond a fringe of saltmarshes and sand-dunes.

This is a manufactured landscape, wrought from unproductive land by human industry, and many of its birds are those that take advantage of human activities. We had come especially to see a very well-known and well-loved bird, the barn owl, which is intimately linked with human habitation. It is a bird of farmland and this has been its downfall. The huge changes in the landscape of lowland Britain over the last four decades have resulted in massive losses of both hunting grounds and nesting places so that the barn owl has disappeared from many of its old haunts. North Norfolk is one of its remaining strongholds and has become the site of an active conservation programme run by Paul Johnson of the Hawk and Owl Trust.

As we drove down the lanes we kept a lookout for barn owls. Although superbly constructed for hunting at night, they are often out in broad daylight during the summer because the short nights coincide with the breeding season, when long hours of hunting are required to secure the food required for the brood of nestling owls. Our destination was a strip of land on the north Norfolk coast where cattle are still raised on grazing marshes. The land has not been tidied up to accommodate juggernaut agricultural machinery, neither have the hedges and ditches been swept aside and replaced with electric fences to marshal the cattle on planted grass leys. The damp, rough marsh pastures are survivors of an untidier age, still divided by weed-filled ditches and straggling hedges, and there are thickets of trees, often of considerable age, and damp hollows choked with reeds and meadowsweet. These

Barn owl hunting grounds at Burnham Norton, not far from Holkham

grazing marshes are a good place for many birds, including barn owls.

The high seawall that separates the grazing marshes from the saltmarshes and the encroaching tide gives a grandstand view so that it is easy to pick up a barn owl, or a marsh harrier, especially when one of these birds of prey lifts above the skyline to show its characteristic shape. The white bodies of gulls may cause momentary confusion with a barn owl, before the absence of rounded wings and large head give truth to the lie. Similarly lapwings sometimes raise expectations for a sighting of a harrier before they turn and show their white bellies. The owl seems to appear out of nowhere; it is suddenly there, silent and light-winged, slowly searching the ground. It checks, turns back for a second look and drops to the ground. Something takes place out of sight, then the owl is back in the air. Now its flight is heavier and it is heading purposefully away from the marsh, carrying its victim back to the waiting brood.

There is often a wait before an owl or harrier turns up but there is plenty to watch in the meantime – families of moorhens and ducks industrious in the dykes and herons flapping heavily overhead in search of a good fishing stance. There were redshank and snipe in the damp grass pasture, reed warblers and reed buntings were still singing and the first flocks of waders, failed breeders probably, had already arrived from distant nesting grounds.

While swallows and martins flew among the grazing cattle, yellow wagtails were running and bobbing to pick up insects disturbed by their hooves and, with even greater cheek, five starlings perched on the back of a lone horse like Old Uncle Tom Cobleigh and all heading for Widdicombe Fair. The horse showed no sign of being aware of forty sharp claws seeking a purchase

A lapwing chick feeding in a muddy pool

Lapwing chick
Burnham marshes
July / 17th /90.

in its hide as it ambled in search of choice grazing. As if at a signal, the starlings flew down in unison, searched the grass with jabbing beaks and flew back to the horse, to continue their slow progress across the marsh and another good chance to feed presented itself.

This delightful pastoral scene with its rich birdlife was once so commonplace it would not have been worth remarking on, but it has almost entirely disappeared from the country. The second purpose of our visit was to see an experiment in land management that is maintaining and modifying traditional farming practices to bring the birds back. The story of the barn owl is intimately linked with the history of agriculture and the conservation of the owl depends on such changes in farming.

History of Agriculture

The countryside of north Norfolk was transformed in the 18th century when its agriculture was hauled out of the Dark Ages. In 1707, Thomas Coke, then a minor but later Earl of Leicester and better known simply as Coke (pronounced Cook) of Norfolk, inherited the family estate of Holkham. It was described as 'a barren, dreary estate, partly heath with a soil of drifting sand, and partly salt marshes, unattractive to the eye as it was unprofitable to the landowner' and it was said that the thin soil could be ploughed by 'rabbits yoked to a pocket knife'. In later years Coke invested heavily in improving his land. Using the methods popularised on the nearby Raynham estate of Viscount 'Turnip' Townshend, as well as advice from agricultural experts such as the cattle breeder Robert Bakewell and William 'Strata' Smith, the pioneer geologist and prototype agricultural consultant who advised on drainage and irrigation, Coke transformed the estate.

Both heath and saltmarsh were attacked. Fifty acres of trees were planted each year until 3000 acres were covered, and Coke eventually had the pleasure of sailing in a ship whose timbers were sawn from his trees. Other stretches of land were enclosed for pasture and arable and at the same time sections of saltmarsh were cut off from the sea by an embankment and drained. The lake in the grounds of Holkham Hall, one mile inland, started as an arm of the sea and two years after draining the surrounding ground was growing corn.

Enclosure of heath and embankment of saltmarsh were not new to Norfolk but Coke's example encouraged his neighbours and in the space of 40 years an area that had grown no wheat became the 'Granary of England'. Holkham was 'a site of splendid timber, rich pasture lands and luxuriant crops' and the estate had the pattern of hedge-girt fields, studded with trees, and small woods that is now as much the traditional landscape of southern England as the contemporary sheep-run moors are of the Scottish Highlands.

The enclosures were not popular with all sections of the community. The nature-loving John Clare wrote in the early nineteenth-century, of his native Northamptonshire:

And birds and trees and flowers without a name
All sighed when lawless laws enclosure came

And again:

Inclosure like a buonaparte let not a thing remain

Until the time of Thomas Coke, farms on the swathe of poor heathland soil running from Cromer to King's Lynn had worked a two-field system in which a crop alternated with a year of lying fallow, rather than the traditional three-field system used on richer land. It was replaced by the Norfolk 4-course system in which there was a rotation of a root crop, originally turnips or swedes, grown as fodder, followed by barley, then a sowing of clover, sainfoin or beans, which were either cut for fodder or ploughed in, and finally a crop of wheat. The root crop replaced the inefficient fallow year and was a bonus because it acted as a break crop for controlling disease and weeds of the cereals and it solved the longstanding problem of winter feed for livestock. The annual slaughter at Martinmas, around the beginning of November, that left only a tiny nucleus of animals to survive the winter half-starved was eliminated and the way was paved for the scientific improvement of farm animals.

In its many variations, the 4-course system became the basis for the Agrarian Revolution, which changed the face of the country socially as well as physically, and it remained so until the post-war mechanical and chemical revolution of agriculture that became 'agribusiness'. The basis of the agrarian revolution was the realisation that yields could be vastly increased by improving the soil. This was accomplished in two ways. First, the fields were enriched with manure derived by feeding the root crop to animals. On the light Norfolk soils, sheep were folded on the crop; on heavier ground, the roots were cut and fed to cattle and the farmyard manure carted back to be spread on the fields. Further fertilisation came from the legumes of the third crop which fixed atmospheric nitrogen. (Sainfoin, meaning 'healthy hay', was introduced from eastern Europe and its deep roots enabled it to flourish on light soils).

The second technique was to build up the structure of thin, sandy soil by marling. Pits were sunk into the fields and the underlying chalky clay or marl dug out and spread. That curmudgeonly reporter of the rural scene, William Cobbett, wrote that he wished 'I had one of these Norfolk men in a coppice in Hampshire or Sussex, and I would show him what *clay* is. Clay is what pots and pans and jugs and tiles are made of; and not soft, whitish stuff that crumbles to pieces in the sun, instead of baking hard as a stone, and which, in dry weather, is to be broken to pieces by nothing short of a sledge-hammer'.

Nevertheless, of all the laborious practices of digging, carting and spreading that the new agriculture demanded, marling must have been the most back-breaking but, once done, the effect was almost permanent. The marl pits can still be seen as circular thickets in the middle of fields. As well as influencing the wild flowers that would grow among the crops in the fields, marling has had an unexpected influence on Norfolk's wildlife which will become apparent later.

Although the new Norfolk system improved yields out of all recognition, a high price was paid for the revolution. Coke spent a fortune converting his land and all over the country there was great distress as the old peasant class was driven out by the enclosures. In the long run the nation benefited by the production of more food and the dispossessed populace, not without further distress, provided the labour force for the Industrial Revolution and settlers for the new colonies.

Crop rotation favours those birds that we think of as farmland birds and whose dwindling populations we now decry. Clare was able to write of the corncrake's song: 'Where is the schoolboy that has not heard that mysterious noise which comes with the spring in the grass and green corn?' It is many years since the distinctive reeling song of this bird of moist meadows was a familiar sound in eastern England.

Yellow wagtails

Ideal barn owl hunting territory

Putting the Clock Back

There was a time when pastures were almost sacred; farm tenancies often contained a clause prohibiting the tenant from ploughing up a pasture. This notion received its death-knell when post-war governments paid grants for pastures to be converted to arable. The result is that there is very little permanent grassland left on southern farms. The grazing marshes of the Norfolk coast are a remnant of an older, less intensive farm system.

The marsh where I had been watching from the top of the dyke had an unusually rich variety of birds because it is part of a National Nature Reserve managed by the Nature Conservancy Council through subsidies to the Holkham estate for modify grazing to benefit the birds. The key is the control of grazing pressure and water level, and the aim is produce the sort of scene that would have been recognised by Coke two hundred years ago. Grazing tenants enter agreements that limit their activities: they may not put cattle on the marshes until late May, grass may not be cut for silage and for hay only after July 1, and they are given a limit on the number of cattle that may be grazed, which, among other effects, reduces the danger of nests being trampled.

The grazing marshes were originally created from the coastal saltmarsh by the building of the seawall and drainage of the enclosed land that was no longer swept by the tides. Drainage channels were cut through the new land and the water table lowered. This was the technique which 'Strata' Smith brought to Holkham, but the levels have dropped since then and the marshes have dried out, especially in the last twenty years. I saw culverts which had been built to carry drainage water under roads and are now high and dry.

The lowering of the water table has been reversed on the Holkham Nature Reserve by the simple process of raising the level of the sluices, in some cases by as much as a metre. One quarter of the ground is allowed to flood during the winter and five per cent is left with standing water through the summer. More water in the ditches and pools attracts ducks and other waterbirds and the damp soil provides good condition for snipe and other waders that probe for worms and insects, but water level must be controlled carefully. If the ground becomes too wet, the invertebrates are killed and the birds go hungry.

The results of the marsh management have been spectacular. In the five years that the Holkham scheme has operated, the numbers of birds nesting in the marshes have increased rapidly. Among waders, snipe have risen from five to 27 pairs, lapwing from 81 to 148 and redshank from eight to 39, while avocets have colonised the marshes for the first time. The outstanding improvement has been among the waterbirds, with gadwall, pochard and shoveler among the newcomers. Meanwhile, three pairs of barn owls have been seen hunting for the voles flourishing in the rich, damp vegetation along ditch banks and in overgrown corners.

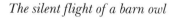

The silent flight of a barn owl

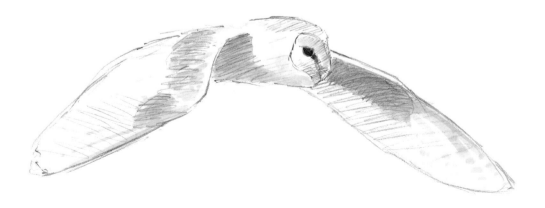

Grazing marshes are only a fragment of Norfolk's agricultural acres and the clock can only be put back in this way on some farms. Huge fields of arable crops are here to stay and the patchwork of little, hedge-girt fields with their rotations of crops will never return. The function of the old crop rotation was two-fold. It kept the land free of weeds and disease, and it fed the crops. Increasingly since 1945, these functions have been usurped by artificial chemicals, such as weed-killers and fertilisers, and crops have been grown according to the profit they will bring. The boom in agriculture has brought more land into cultivation, at the expense of woodlands, wetlands and heaths, and so destroyed their birds, but it has also changed the habitat of farmland itself so that the many birds that used to flourish in arable or pasture have diminished. Agricultural policy and farming technology ultimately determine the shape of the countryside.

In all, the effect of the first agrarian revolution was to create a greater diversity of habitats which supported a greater variety of bird life but the second has transformed the countryside into a few, simple habitats which support fewer birds. The British Trust for Ornithology's Common Bird Census has shown how the large flocks of finches that once brought colour and movement to the rural scene are now almost a thing of the past. There are too few weeds and harvesting is too efficient to provide the seeds they need. Moreover, a long-term survey has demonstrated the amazing decline of the grey partridge. We are used to peregrines, kites, divers and greenshanks being rare birds but it is a shock to find that common, almost garden, birds are fading from our everyday lives.

The numbers of partridges started to drop 100 years ago, but they have plummeted in the last three decades and grey partridges, once shot in their millions, are comparatively rare birds. The first problem is that partridge nests are extremely vulnerable to predators. Foxes kill the sitting hens and stoats, rats, hedgehogs and crows steal the eggs. Dogs taken for walks along hedgerows can easily cause partridges to desert the nest. Formerly, gamekeepers kept predators and dog-walking under control. I have just read of an experiment by the Game Conservancy which showed a very significant difference in the numbers of partridges in keepered and unkeepered areas. The general decrease in keepering is therefore responsible for the early decline of the grey partridge. The more recent slump is due to the increasing use of chemicals on farms, first herbicides and then insecticides. These kill the insects and other tiny animals which partridge chicks depend on for the first few weeks of life.

As a result of its researches into partridges, the Game Conservancy found that breeding can be improved with a small change to farming practice to create Conservation Headlands. First, a narrow strip, perhaps a ditch bank or the border of a hedge, is left uncultivated as a nesting place and a sanctuary for insects. Then a second strip is rotovated and left bare to prevent invasion of the crop by weeds, but the main measure is to restrict the spraying of a 6-metre border (the width of a spray boom) around the field to control only the most troublesome weeds. Research has shown that this treatment will let the partridge population recover for a yield reduction of less than half a per cent in a 40-acre field.

There are also encouraging signs that the conservation headland scheme could be one road to salvation for many more kinds hard-pressed farmland wildlife. Field edges have erupted in bright borders of colour where the seeds of once common wild flowers – viper's bugloss, mignonette, poppies and night-flowering catchfly – have lain dormant for years. These support the insects, spiders and other animals which partridges and other birds need to rear their young. The advantage to the farmer is the increase in the number of his valuable gamebirds and the savings in expensive sprays.

Old Hush Wing – the Farmer's Friend

The barn owl's habit of hunting by day during the breeding season gives the ornithologist a marvellous chance of watching a nocturnal predator at work. As the owl quarters a field or flies slowly along a roadside verge in the gathering gloom, you can imagine the scene in a few hours time when the

Barn owls hunting

human eye can barely make out the white form with the blunt-headed owl's outline in the gathering gloom.

My particular pleasure in watching barn owls comes from knowing something of the physical capability of the species and so trying to get inside the mind of an owl while it is hunting and appreciate what it is doing. This is possible because the barn owl's senses of eyesight and hearing and the role they play in the capture of prey has been investigated in captive owls (made possible by the ease with they can be reared and tamed).

It is easier to see what an owl is doing when it is hunting from a perch. (When in owl country, keep a watch on lines of fence posts. If one looks a little taller than the rest, check whether the difference is due to an owl perched on it.) The eyes of an owl face forwards, as is usual among predators, to give it the good binocular vision required for pinpointing a target. Judging distance is aided by the owl's habit of bobbing and weaving its head, even turning it on one side. The owl is a picture of excited curiosity, as if it is trying to get a better look from the back of a crowd, but the true function seems to be to focus on an object from slightly different angles to help the brain compute the range.

The flexibility of movement is also necessary because the eyeball is so large that it cannot swivel inside the skull, and the owl has to turn its head to look around. The disadvantage is that owls have a narrow field of vision and, unlike other birds which have good all-round vision, a barn owl can be surprised by a stealthy approach from behind. If it is staring intently at something on the ground below its perch, it is possible to creep to within 15-20 feet before it takes flight.

It is impossible, of course, for an owl to see in pitch darkness, but it is never totally dark in the countryside. Even on a cloudy, moonless night enough light seeps down from the stars to illuminate the scene for animals with very sensitive eyes. And nowadays there is always a loom of light from houses and roads. It is not fully understood how an owl's eye is adapted for night vision but the large size of the eyeball is believed to give a large image on the retina which can be processed by the sense cells more effectively than the smaller images of diurnal birds. One of the surprising findings of recent research is that the light-collecting ability of an owl's eye is not much better than ours. So how can a barn owl hunt when we are left blundering into hedges and falling into ditches? The answer seems to lie in other aspects of its visual system such as the sensitivity of the retina to very low light levels.

What exactly can be seen does, however, depend on the amount of light and hunting must be much easier during the day. The grey-brown fur of mice and voles is inconspicuous at the best of times and they live among dense herbage, keeping to runs whenever possible so that there is often little more than a flash of a small body or the wavering of stems and leaves to give away their position. When a small mammal ventures to expose itself, it

About to pounce

proceeds with extreme caution and alertness. The slightest alarm prompts a dash to safety or an instant freeze. The owl's eyes are designed to detect movement and, if the mammal can freeze before it is spotted, it has a good chance of escaping.

When the owl is hunting by flying over the field, it looks down to scan the ground below, bringing its binocular vision into play, and checks at intervals, hanging on winnowing wings like a kestrel and sometimes turning back to verify a suspicion. Much must depend on the owl's experience to discern the curve of a back, a glimpse of an ear or the gleam of a beady eye caught in the moonlight. There will be other movements catching its eye: an earthworm dragging a leaf into its burrow or feeling around in search of a mate, a beetle scurrying over the ground or a moth shivering its wings to warm up for a night flight. Unlike a tawny owl or a little owl, which are less particular, the barn owl will not bother to catch such trifles, unless it is an inexperienced youngster.

Much must depend on getting as sharp a view as possible. A barn owl scanning for prey must be like a birdwatcher searching for that elusive warbler, continually focussing his binoculars in and out to sharpen the bird's image and make it stand out. Then, the target located and identified, the owl must keep it in focus; failure may mean more than a missed meal, the hunter could injure itself through misjudgement. Although barn owls hunt close to the ground, they power down headfirst towards their prey in a split second. Their eyes can change focus very rapidly, from a longsighted scanning of the far distance for navigation to shortsighted homing in on prey, beyond the capacity of the human eye. Try reading this page while swinging to and fro. It is not too difficult until your face comes within inches of the print. One advantage for the owl is that its eyes maintain a sharp image at ranges that leave us blearily staring at an out of focus image.

As darkness gathers, spotting and tracking prey by sight becomes more difficult but the barn owl, like most predators, does not rely totally on a single sense. The barn owl's hearing is also extremely acute. The facial disc surrounded by the heart-shaped ruff is an efficient sound-collecting device. The feathers of the disc are loose, almost threadbare, to let sound waves pass through, while the ruff feathers are stiff and densely packed to form a sound reflector that helps direct sound into the ears. The disc feathers hide a pair of ear-flaps directly in front of the ear openings. Our ear-flaps are more than ornaments and hangers for rings and spectacles, because the arrangement of folds improves our ability to localise sounds, but the barn owl's ear-flaps have the refinement of being asymmetrically positioned, one higher than the other, as a further aid to sound localisation.

When an owl is swinging its head from side to side, is it trying to see or hear better? It is probably trying to do both, with the emphasis on hearing as it gets darker. As far as I know, owls have never been fitted with blindfolds or ear muffs, like dolphins, so that they are forced to rely either on sight or sound to find their prey, but an experiment has been done in a blacked-out room to test their hearing. The owl could pounce on a mouse released on the floor, provided that it was rustling through leaves. One rustle was enough for the owl to pinpoint the mouse but the attack was slower and less certain in total darkness, and the final strike was more accurate if there was some light.

Owls do not live in a laboratory but in the vastly more complicated and imperfect real world. We can imagine the owl patrolling or waiting on a perch with eyes and ears straining for clues of what is happening on the ground below. A mouse crunching a grass stem or two shrews chasing and squeaking in a border dispute, a young mole blundering blindly in search of a free space to dig its tunnels or a frog croaking at the edge of a pond are living on borrowed time. This may give the impression of a one-sided relationship

Swifts in flight

between predator and prey but life is by no means easy for the predator. Bad weather makes hunting difficult and Paul Johnson said that he had seen an owl hunting in a gale by hugging the ground in the lee of a thick hedge, until it reached a gate when the blast of air swept it away. Hunting from a perch is a better option but trying to locate prey while being swung around like a balloon on a string must be difficult. Heavy rain may stop an owl's hunting altogether, unless it finds a barn where it can hunt mice under cover. Not only does its plumage get waterlogged easily, the noise of the rain drowns the sounds of its prey.

Aerial Birds

Our visit to the marsh was well-timed. It was a hot, breezy day in late July and the birds were on the wing in search of food for their families. There was a good chance of seeing a barn owl because the rodent population of these wet grazing marshes attracted three neighbouring pairs of owls which were likely to visit at any time in the late afternoon.

While waiting for an owl to put in an appearance, we watched for an even rarer predator. The marsh harrier is eye-catchingly different from the starlings, lapwings, pigeons and gulls flying to and fro across the marsh because of its immensely slow, flap and glide flight. The species has had the chequered career typical of our birds of prey. Once abundant in extensive reedbeds, it went to decline as drainage schemes took hold of the country in the 18th century and crashed with the onslaught by gamekeepers, egg collectors and taxidermists in the 19th century. It was extinct in Britain as a breeding

A female marsh harrier quartering the ground as she hunts

bird by 1900. Successful nesting started again in 1928, with a good nucleus building up in the Norfolk Broads. Then the pesticide crisis of the 1960s nearly wiped it out but numbers have again built up, starting at the RSPB reserve at Minsmere. There are now around 60 pairs, mainly in eastern counties and an encouraging sign is that they now nest in small reedbeds or even in arable crops so that there is hope that their expansion will not be limited by a shortage of suitable habitat.

The marsh harrier will appear as a darker version of the barn owl because the two birds have much in common in their appearance and hunting habits. Although not so obvious in the marsh harrier as in the hen harrier, the harriers have a facial disc and ruff similar to those of owls. The eyes are also set forward to give good binocular vision. Both features are examples of convergent evolution – where unrelated animals develop similar characteristics. The ears are used for hunting hidden prey – the owls' victims are concealed by darkness and the harriers' by dense vegetation. The harriers are long-legged for reaching into the vegetation to grasp prey and, in another example of convergence, barn owls are noticeably longer-legged than many other owls.

Both marsh harrier and barn owl hunt by quartering low over the ground. They head into the wind for extra lift so they can keep their speed over the ground to a minimum and peer and listen at leisure. The harrier flies lower and slower than the owl and often disappears below the level of the reeds. Its flight is more buoyant and more time is spent gliding, with the wings in a shallow V. The harrier has the same long wings as a barn owl but the primary feathers at the tips separate into fingers whereas the barn owl's wings are rounded. Long wings with a large surface area are the key to the slow flight these birds employ when hunting but the splayed fingers of the harrier, reminiscent of the soaring vultures, give it an advantage over the owl. Each 'finger' acts as a tiny winglet and helps to improve the efficiency of the wing so that the harrier can fly extremely slowly without stalling.

The lazy flight of the owl and harrier contrasted with the flurry and dash of the swallows, house martins and swifts that were the most conspicuous birds over the marshes. (It is annoying that, while the swallows and martins can be lumped together as hirundines, the superficially similar swift is so distantly related that there is no common collective name for all these long-winged, aerial insect-eaters.) They were everywhere, swarming over the pastures and darting among the cattle, working their way slowly into the wind, then turning and slipping back the way they came. I was reminded of folklore I heard as a child: if swallows fly low it is going to rain. It cannot be true; they were skimming the pasture and we were in the middle of a long drought! It is the same with cows lying down. Keep an eye on them as you drive down the lanes and you will find the forecast is nearly always showers with bright intervals!

The streamlined shapes of swallows, martins and swifts with their narrow, pointed sweptback wings faired into the bullet-shaped body are ideal for

House martins nest high in the stonework of Holkham Hall

high-speed flight. Yet, despite the contrast with the blunt-winged barn owl and marsh harrier, these birds depend on flying slowly for catching flying insects as much as the larger birds do for pouncing on rodents. Both groups of birds have to stay airborne for long periods and must fly economically and even the swift is not so speedy as its name and reputation would suggest. On this windy day, the swallows were manoeuvring with hardly a wingbeat as they tacked across the wind.

It seems that the grazing marshes are as rich in flying insects as they are in rodents but, for these aerial hunters, the significance of the 17th century agricultural improvement lay more in the building that accompanied it. From cattle sheds to the Palladian magnificence of Holkham Hall, buildings have provided swallows, house martins and swifts with nesting places. The natural nesting places for these birds is cliffs, although swifts are known to use old woodpecker holes in trees, so there can have been few of these birds in primaeval north Norfolk. Where the barn owl has taken advantage of tree-planting to extend its range, so the aerial hunters have benefited from buildings. Surprisingly, they have not suffered from poisons picked up in their insect prey and have remained numerous throughout the era of chemical agriculture.

Young Barn owls — 6 weeks old.
North Norfolk.

Holkham — North Norfolk
June 20th /90

young Barn owl.
almost five weeks old

Holkham - N. Norfolk.
28th/June/90.

same owl as 20/June.
down almost all gone.

Although their plumage is beautifully marked, their heart-shaped face is the most striking feature of the Barn Owl – particularly when young

The swallow has declined, partly through the changes in its African winter home that also halved the population of the sand martin, and partly from the loss and conversion of farm buildings.

What has Happened to the Barn Owl?

The barn owl, hunting over fields and flying to its nest in a barn, church or hayrick, was once a common sight. The species had benefited from the felling of the primaeval forest and the creation of the man-made agricultural landscape. Fields and stores of harvested crops encouraged its rodent prey and buildings provided nest-sites, but the barn owl was not able to cope with the recent transformation of its habitat into a single continuous seedbed. The barn owl population of Britain and Ireland has dropped by 70 percent over the last 60 years to around 5000 pairs. In contrast, there are 75,000 pairs of tawny owls, which two centuries ago were regarded as less abundant than barn owls.

These figures were revealed in a survey by the Hawk and Owl Trust, which also uncovered the causes of the dramatic decline. The Agrarian Revolution and the Enclosures created rich pastures, stubble fields, hedgerows and well-filled barns where small mammals flourished. The diet of barn owls is predominately small mammals, especially field voles and to a lesser extent other voles, wood mice, common shrews and rats, so the barn owl easily qualifies as the 'farmer's friend'. It had long been the custom to provide barns with small windows let into the gable ends to encourage barn owls to nest but the emerging popularity of field sports in 19th century Britain ignorantly turned barn owls into vermin. Egg-collecting and the craze for stuffed birds added to the slaughter and the Dickensian winters of the latter half of the 19th century were hard for a bird at the northern end of its range.

There was some recovery in barn owl numbers in the 20th century as all these problems eased, but after 1945 there came the intensification of agriculture and the introduction of pesticides which were easily passed on to the owls by seed-eating rodents. Worse still, the winter climate again deteriorated. Cold weather does not kill barn owls if they are well-fed, but a blanket of snow that hides their rodent prey does. Twenty days snow cover in a winter appears to be a critical level for their survival. In the 40 years before 1940 this occurred only once, but it has happened 21 times since. One result is that the barn owl has become a lowland bird with its remaining population concentrated in the river valleys of the south.

These snowy winters coincided with the introduction of combine harvesters and the disappearance of ricks and stacks that provided a rich source of rodents in winter as well as valuable nest-sites. The increasing disappearance of barns and old hollow trees also robbed the owls of shelter.

A hunting barn owl

Conservation Efforts

With food and shelter disappearing and a growing toll from feeding on poisoned rats or colliding with cars and lorries, the barn owl could have become yet another species doomed to extreme rarity if a vigorous conservation programme had not swung into action.

Bruce chose the barn owls of Norfolk partly so that we could inspect the work of the Hawk and Owl Trust in the Holkham area where Paul Johnson is working with local landowners and farmers to make the country again fit for barn owls.

One step is to ensure that the existing pairs have places to nest. Contrary to what might be expected, most barn owls in the south and east of England nest in hollow trees – of 68 sites found by Paul, 59 have been in old trees, especially elm and ash. Several reasons could explain why more trees than barns are used. Barn owls in northern and western counties are probably driven to use barns because they provide better protection from rain. The south-east is drier and trees are larger and more likely to develop cavities large enough for an barn owl's nest. Furthermore, Norfolk barns do not have the deep ledges needed for a nest and owls occupy them only when there are piles of straw bales to provide a safe site.

Many suitable trees have disappeared with the general clearing and tidying of the countryside and there is a continuing attrition as old trees blow over or disappear where roads are widened and houses built. Those owls that do nest in the traditional site are being evicted by the vogue for converting barns and other outbuildings into dwellings. The solution is to provide nestboxes. Paul took us to see a nestbox in the roof of a flint and brick steading and as we approached two owls flew silently out of the door and away over the fields. The lack of noise was amazing; a woodpigeon disturbed from its roost would make an enormous clatter. We entered to find four downy white caricatures of barn owls gazing down, silently alert. The box had been there for two years before the owls moved in; one of the pair was a young adult that had come from a nest in the next village.

Paul brought the owlets down to ring and Bruce perched one on his knee to quickly sketch. I took the opportunity to get a close look at the feathering of the facial disc and ruff. The owlet took this attention with the equanimity of a placid cat. Paul explained that two or three of these owlets would fail to survive beyond their first year and any owls that reached adulthood would have a further life-expectancy of three or four years, perhaps five at the most. So the second, and perhaps most important, part of his conservation work is to secure their habitat.

Coke's Norfolk would have been ideal for barn owls and the appreciation of earlier generations of farmers for their efforts at keeping down rats and mice is shown by the number of owl windows in old barns. Like many other

Winter can be a difficult time for barn owls

animals, barn owls were only incidental victims of the intensifying post-war agriculture. Many farmers were well disposed towards barn owls, but only in a passive way. The success of the Hawk and Owl Trust's programme is that they are now becoming positive towards the owls, for instance by stopping to think before putting the chainsaw to an old tree, which may have an owl nesting in it, or before putting down rat poison in the barn, where an owl may hunt.

Encouragement for barn owls comes from erecting nestboxes in farmland which will help lure them away from the danger of roads. The thickets that have grown over the old marl pits are ideal for the purpose. Some farmers are even letting the hedges grow taller so that barn owls are forced to cross lanes at heights that will carry them over passing traffic. Pauls' efforts to help barn owls in Norfolk have also benefited from the Game Conservancy's headland conservation plan.

It has been found that barn owls can live in a completely linear habitat where the pastures and other open habitats have gone. A linear habitat can be a roadside verge, a river bank or an uncultivated border of a field. One pair of barn owls needs a 6m headland strip 9-15 miles long. The essential ingredients are enough rough herbage to support plenty of rodents and a place to nest. Sometimes Paul can carry out remedial surgery to a hollow tree make it suitable for owls, perhaps by blocking gaps at the bottom of the hollow and providing a bed of sawdust. Otherwise, a nest box is provided. A good example of what can be done is shown by Paul's experience in the north-western corner of Norfolk where roadside avenues of beech trees were cleared during the war for the safety of low-flying bombers. This created a large gap in barn owl distribution which he has successfully plugged with the aid of nestboxes.

But will farmers want to go to the trouble of encouraging barn owls unless they simply want the pleasure of their company? Paul believes they will because Old Hushwing is a practical friend. Over the last 20 years wood mice have become a serious pest in sugarbeet, which is an important crop in Norfolk. A group of mice can clear rows of newly drilled seed in the course of a night's feeding. The problem is most serious when large numbers of mice have survived the winter, but they will attract the owls to hunt in the fields. With no cover, the mice will be very vulnerable to a silent pounce.

GENERAL READING

Brown, Leslie. *British Birds of Prey*. Collins. 1976

Brown, Philip and George Waterston. *The Return of the Osprey*. Collins. 1962.
(Includes The Return of the Black-tailed Godwit.)

Bunn, D.S., A.B. Warburton and R.D.S. Wilson. *The Barn Owl*. T. & A.D. Poyser.
1982

Condry, William M. *The Natural History of Wales*. Collins. 1981

Darling, F. Fraser and J. Morton Boyd. *The Highlands and Islands*. Collins. 1964

Fuller, R.J. *Bird Habitats in Britain*. T. & A.D. Poyser. 1982

Hale, W.G. *Waders*. Collins. 1980

Hammond, Nicholas (ed.). *R.S.P.B. Nature Reserves*. R.S.P.B. 1983

Nature Conservancy Council. *The Flow Country. The Peatlands of Caithness and
Sutherland*. N.C.C. 1988

Nature Conservancy Council. *Birds, Bogs and Forestry. The Peatlands of Caithness and
Sutherland*. N.C.C. 1987

Nethersole-Thompson, Desmond. *The Greenshank*. Collins. 1951

Nethersole-Thompson, Desmond and Maimie Nethersole-Thompson. *Waders, their
Breeding, Haunts and Watchers*. T. & A.D. Poyser. 1986

Rackham, Oliver. *The History of the Countryside*. Dent. 1986

Ratcliffe, Derek. *The Peregrine*. T. & A.D. Poyser. 1980

R.S.P.B. *Conservation Reviews 1987, 1988, 1989*. R.S.P.B.

Ruskin, John. *Modern Painters* (edited and abridged by David Barrie). André
Deutsch. 1987

Shawyer, Colin R. *The Barn Owl in the British Isles. Its past, present and future*. The
Hawk Trust. 1987.

Tansley, A.G. *Britain's Green Mantle*. George Allen & Unwin. 1968 (2nd edition)

Treleaven, R.B. *Private Life of the Peregrine Falcon*. Headland. 1977

Webb, Nigel. *Heathlands*. Collins. 1986

ACKNOWLEDGEMENTS

The author and artist would like to acknowledge the many people who have generously assisted us with our fieldwork, with hospitality and with assistance on our travels.

Cornwall

Dan Driscoll, Dick Treleaven, David Woolcock (The Rare and Endangered Bird Breeding Centre, Paradise Park)

Flows

Roger Cadwallader (Fountain Forestry), Roy Dennis (RSPB), Angus Ross, Bruce Sandison, Dr D Thompson and Dr Richard Lindsay (Nature Conservancy Council)

Wales

Gwyn and Mona Lloyd, Tony Pickup and Peter Davies (RSPB)

Washes

Don Revett and Dr Julian Hector (Wildfowl and Wetland Trust), Josh Scott (who sadly died during the making of the programmes)

Heaths

Martin Auld and Colin Bibby (RSPB) and Stephen Lyman-Dixon

Norfolk

Alan Hale, David Henshilwood (Nature Conservancy Council), Paul Johnson (Hawk and Owl Trust), Rod Playford and John Smith

David Cobham, Avie Littler, Helga Dowie, Mike Potts and the crew from Central TV Facilities; Chris Harbard, Ian Dawson and the staff at the headquarters of the R.S.P.B.; and Sue Shephard at Channel 4.

The author acknowledges permission from the family of Desmond Nethersole-Thompson to quote from his book *The Greenshank* and from Lady Scott to quote from the imaginary letter by Sir Peter Scott reprinted in the Wildfowl and Wetland Trust's magazine *Wildfowl World*.

The television programmes on which this book is based were produced for Channel Four Television by Avie Littler Associates Ltd.

INDEX